THE CREEK WAR, 1813–14

THE CREEK WAR, 1813–14

Richard D. Blackmon

CIS0056

Published in 2025 by
CASEMATE PUBLISHERS
1950 Lawrence Road, Havertown, PA 19083, USA
and
47 Church Street, Barnsley, S70 2AS, UK

Main text, Center of Military History, United States Army, Washington, D.C., 2013
Boxed text and timeline by Chris McNab © Casemate Publishers 2025

Paperback edition: ISBN 978-1-63624-550-8
Digital edition: ISBN 978-1-63624-551-5

A CIP record for this book is available from the British Library.

All rights reserved. No part of this book may be reproduced or transmitted in any form or by any means, electronic or mechanical including photocopying, recording or by any information storage and retrieval system, without permission from the publisher in writing.

Maps by Myriam Bell
Design by Myriam Bell
Printed and bound in the United Kingdom by Short Run Press

For a complete list of Casemate titles, please contact:

CASEMATE PUBLISHERS (US)
Telephone (610) 853-9131
Fax (610) 853-9146
Email: casemate@casematepublishers.com
www.casematepublishers.com

CASEMATE PUBLISHERS (UK)
Telephone (0)1226 734350
Email: casemate@casemateuk.com
www.casemateuk.com

Front cover image, bottom right: Troop positions for the battle of Horseshoe Bend. (Library of Congress, Geography and Map Division)

The Publisher's authorised representative in the EU for product safety is Authorised Rep Compliance Ltd., Ground Floor, 71 Lower Baggot Street, Dublin D02 P593, Ireland.
www.arccompliance.com

Contents

Timeline................... 6

Introduction 9

Battle of Burnt Corn 20

The Fort Mims Massacre......... 25

Tennessee and Andrew Jackson 29

The Georgia Militia and the Offensive
  from the East.................. 40

The Mississippi Militia................. 44

Jackson and the Tennessee Volunteers ... 49

A New Year and a Renewed Effort....... 52

Andrew Jackson and the Final
  Campaign 61

Analysis 73

Further Reading 77

Index 79

Timeline

The Creek War can trace its origins to 1805, when the Ocmulgee River became the boundary between the Creek Nation and Georgia, with a "civilization program" imposed on the Creeks. 1812 saw several Creek attacks on white families and travelers in Tennessee, and, importantly, the outbreak of the War of 1812 with the British. British and Spanish support for the Creeks would soon be forthcoming. Prior to the Creek War proper, the Creek Nation was involved in civil war, before Colonel Caller's militia army was defeated by Red Stick forces at the battle of Burnt Corn Creek in July 1813. A month later, Red Stick warriors massacred 560 militia and civilians at Fort Mims, setting the tone for the atrocities and brutality that characterized the war on both sides. From November 9, 1813, with the battle of Talladega, the war was marked by a series of inexorable Creek defeats, culminating in the decisive battle of Horseshoe Bend in March 1814. The terms of the Treaty of Fort Jackson forced on the defeated Creeks by Major General Andrew Jackson were unduly harsh, with a cruel addendum of the Creeks being forced to cede twenty-three million acres of land, earning Jackson the moniker "Sharp Knife."

1805 — The Ocmulgee River becomes the boundary between the Creek Nation and Georgia. Federal officials also institute a "civilization program" for the Native Americans.

1811 — As tensions rise with Britain, the U.S. government authorizes the further expansion of the Federal Road to facilitate the rapid movement of military forces to the Gulf Coast. Tecumseh seeks to expand his pan-American Indian alliance into the South.

1812 — There are a number of Creek attacks on white families and travelers in Tennessee.

1813

January 8 — Responding to fears about potential Spanish support for Britain in the South, Major General Andrew Jackson raises two thousand volunteers to reinforce New Orleans and to attack the Spanish, although the operation is later called off.

June–July — Factions within the Creek Nation result in a slide into a Native American civil war.

July 13 — Tennessee's Governor William Blount writes to Georgia Governor David B. Mitchell requesting that he organize an army of fifteen hundred militiamen for operations in the Creek territory.

July 25 — Colonel James Caller leads a militia army against the Red Stick forces.

July 27 — Battle of Burnt Corn Creek, the first engagement of the Creek War. The militia are forced to retreat.

▲ This view give a good impression of the breadth and terrain of the Mobile River. The photograph was taken from the site of the former Fort Stoddert near Mount Vernon, Alabama. The 3d Infantry Regiment was deployed to the fort following the Fort Mims massacre. (Altairisfar/PD, via Wikimedia Commons)

August 30	A large force of Red Stick warriors, commanded by Peter McQueen and William Weatherford, storm and take Fort Mims north of Mobile, Alabama, massacring more than 560 militia and civilians.
November 3	Battle of Tallushatchee. A 900-strong dragoon unit under Brigadier General John Coffee destroys a Red Stick force of nearly 200 warriors and civilians north of Alexandria, Alabama.
November 9	Battle of Talladega. In Mississippi Territory, Brigadier General Jackson inflicts another disproportionate defeat on Red Stick forces.
November 10	East Tennessee militia under Brigadier General James White kill sixty-nine Creek warriors in the Hillabee towns.
c. November 15	Brigadier General Ferdinand L. Claiborne oversees construction of a fort on the Alabama River at Weatherford's Bluff.
November 24	Georgian militia forces cross the Chattahoochee River and establish Fort Mitchell as a forward supply center.
November 29	Battle of Autosee. The Georgia militia destroy the Creek towns of Autossee and Tallasee.
December 23	Battle of Holy Ground/Econochaca. A major clash between U.S. militia/federal troops and Red Stick warriors results in a victory for neither side, most of the Native Americans escaping encirclement.

1814

January 17	Jackson leads his force south toward the Tallapoosa River. He is subsequently compelled to withdraw in the face of harassing Red Stick attacks.
January 27	The Red Sticks attack Camp Defiance during the predawn hours. Supported by their artillery, the Georgians gain the advantage and the Red Sticks withdraw.
March 27	Battle of Horseshoe Bend. A large force of U.S. troops inflict a decisive defeat on the Red Sticks near Dadeville, Alabama.
August 9	Andrew Jackson compels the Creek to sign the Treaty of Fort Jackson.

Introduction

About a year after the United States declared war on Great Britain in June 1812, a conflict erupted in the American South that would become known as the Creek War. The Creek War was a complicated affair. It was both a civil war between two factions within the Creek Nation and an international struggle in which the United States, Spain, Britain, and other American Indian tribes played a part. America's ultimate victory in the conflict helped shape the outcome of the broader war with Britain and gained significant new territory for white settlement in the American South.

▼ Benjamin Hawkins.
(New York Public Library)

Strategic Setting

After the end of the American Revolution in 1783, Georgia experienced an explosion in population, and many new settlers looked for opportunities to acquire land in the western part of the state, largely occupied by Creek American Indians. Their homeland included riverside towns, crop fields, and hunting grounds that extended into what is now Alabama. The Creeks were historically and culturally divided into two groups: the Upper Creek towns, located primarily along the Coosa and Tallapoosa Rivers and their tributaries in what is now Alabama, and the Lower Creek towns, found in the Flint and Chattahoochee river valleys of western Georgia.

Before 1790, Georgia made several treaties in which Lower Creek headmen ceded the land between the Ogeechee and Oconee Rivers to the state, but

The Creek War, 1813–14

The Southeast of the United States was a troubled region in the first two decades of the 19th century. Here we see the opening page of the Constitution of East Florida, a document written in March 1812 by the Patriot Army after they gained control of Fernandina, following a government-approved invasion of Florida. (PD, via Wikimedia Commons)

Upper Creek leaders refused to acknowledge the validity of these agreements. This disagreement resulted in frequent Creek attacks on Georgia settlers in the disputed territory. In 1790, the U.S. government made its first treaty with the Creeks, one in which both Lower and Upper Creek leadership participated. In subsequent treaties, the Creeks ceded more lands to the United States until the Ocmulgee River became the boundary between the Creek Nation and Georgia in 1805.

Federal officials also instituted a "civilization program," implemented and promoted by the American Indian agent for the United States, Benjamin Hawkins. His program of teaching agriculture and "domestic arts" to the Creeks succeeded primarily with the Lower Creeks. Their conversion from a hunting/bartering economy to a market economy produced great wealth among many of them, particularly those of mixed-blood ancestry who claimed a white father (usually a trader or merchant) and a Creek mother. This, however, caused resentment between those economically successful Lower Creeks and many Upper Creeks who opposed assimilation.

Hawkins created a governing body for all Creeks, the National Council, which intentionally circumvented the previous polity of town headmen. The council redistributed political power from the town level to the national level. Benjamin Hawkins naturally exercised great influence over who sat on the council and selected those Creeks sympathetic to the United States. Traditionalist Creeks resented the National Council and sought to eliminate it.

► *William McIntosh* from McKenney & Hall, *History of the Indian Tribes of North America* (1838–1844). (University of Cincinnati Libraries Digital Collections)

The Creek War, 1813–14

Further cause for division occurred when the United States sought to extend the Federal Road through Creek territory to connect Georgia with the Mississippi Territory (Map 1). William McIntosh, a powerful Lower Creek leader with strong ties to the U.S. government, convinced those Creeks opposing the road to support the project in an 1805 treaty. Though the pathway provided some Creeks with a source of income from tolls and businesses along its route, the track also brought a flood of settlers to the Mississippi Territory, adding another cause of friction between white people and American Indians. As tensions between the United

▶ Tecumseh. (Library of Congress)

◀ Tenskwatawa ("The Open Door") was the brother of the great warrior Tecumseh. As a religious teacher of the Shawnee people, he was known as "The Prophet," but he also led Native Americans in resistance to U.S. encroachments. (Smithsonian American Art Museum)

TECUMSEH.

The Creek War, 1813–14

States and Great Britain increased, in 1811 the U.S. government authorized the further expansion of the Federal Road to facilitate the rapid movement of military forces to the Gulf Coast. The National Council Creeks supported the project while traditionalists opposed it.

The United States had legitimate concerns regarding the possibility of foreign military action in the region. Since the beginning of colonization in North America, European powers had regarded the Gulf Coast as a key asset. In the post-Revolutionary years, the British had attempted to stem the westward flow of American settlers by supporting American Indians from coastal trading posts. Spain, in possession of the Floridas, also had an uneasy relationship with the United States, and had long sought to influence local American Indians to shield its territory from American encroachment.

Into this turbulent situation in the fall of 1811 came Tecumseh. A Shawnee warrior from north of the Ohio River, Tecumseh and his brother Tenkswatawa ("The Prophet") had forged an alliance between the British and many northern tribes. Tecumseh advocated an armed uprising by all American Indians against the encroachments of American settlers. In the summer of 1811, Tecumseh sought to expand his pan-American Indian alliance into the South. He first visited the Chickasaws. Rebuffed, he continued on to the Choctaws, but one of their chiefs, Pushmataha, was a staunch friend of the United States and countered Tecumseh's

▼ A view of the outer works of Fort Charlotte in Mobile, Alabama. It was originally a French fort, Fort Condé, built in the 1720s, but its name changed to Fort Charlotte in 1813. (Cheburashka007/ CC BY-SA 4.0, via Wikimedia Commons)

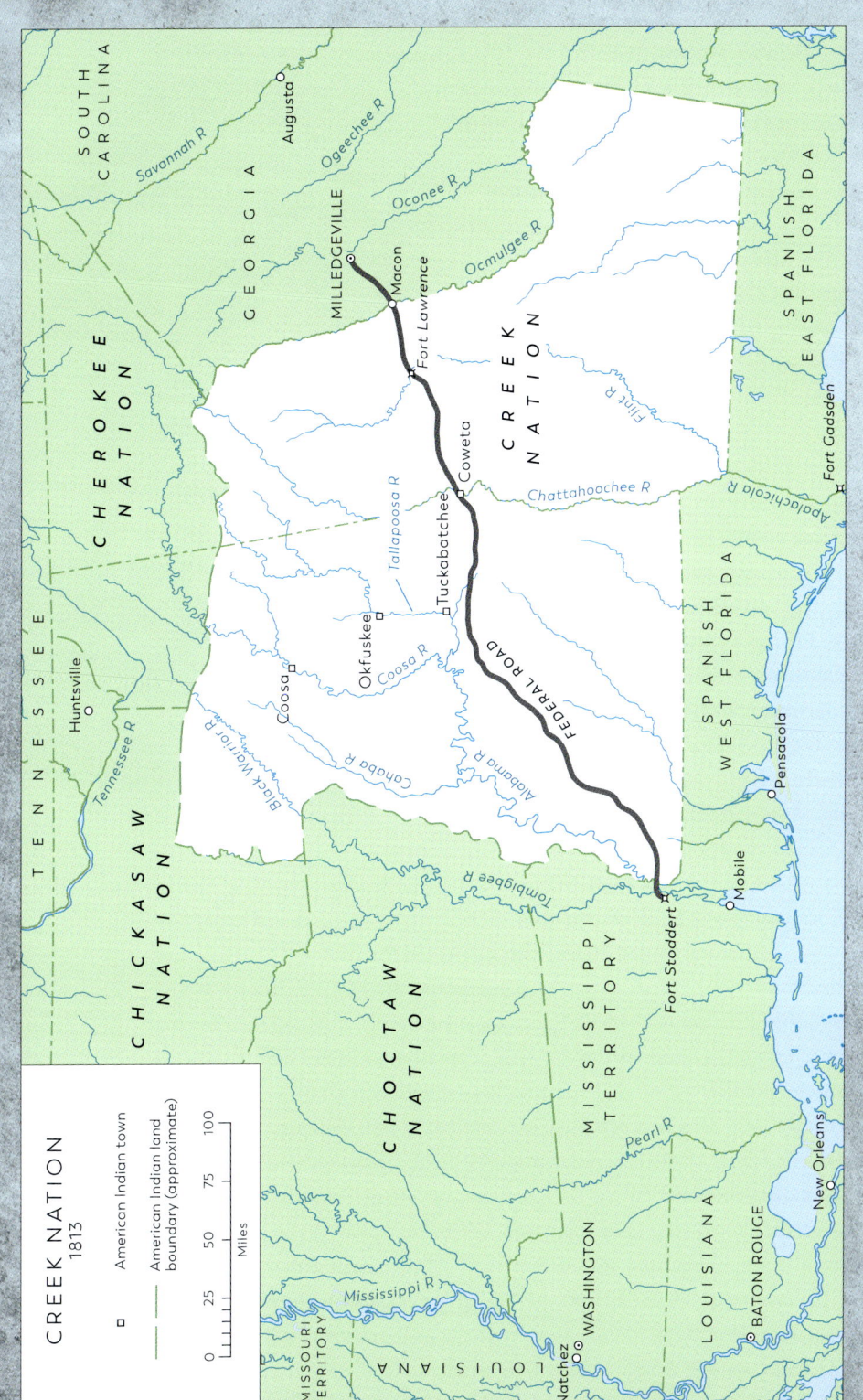

▲ Map 1

The Creek War, 1813–14

efforts. He then ventured on to the Creek Nation, where he encountered a more receptive audience. Admonishing his adherents not to strike until the pan-American Indian alliance was ready to act in unison, Tecumseh returned to his home in the North before the end of the year.

In the spring of 1812, a few of Tecumseh's Creek followers killed several white travelers on the Federal Road. Hawkins responded by calling a meeting of the National Council in June. The council condemned the perpetrators to death and sent out warriors to carry out the sentences. That same month, news filtered into the backcountry that the United States had declared war on Great Britain and that a party of Creeks, led by Little Warrior, returning from a meeting with Tecumseh in the North, killed two white families along the Duck River in Tennessee. Small-scale attacks against settlers continued sporadically during the remainder of 1812, as did condemnation and retaliatory justice by the National Council. A serious rift soon developed in the Creek Nation. One faction consisted of those leaders who received monetary emoluments from the United States, who supported the National Council, and who rejected Tecumseh's call to war. Members of the other faction, known as Red Sticks, disliked the council's challenge to local autonomy, resented the growing influence of white culture at the expense of traditional values, and embraced Tecumseh's political vision and the Prophet's religious teachings. As the year wore on, the animosity between these two factions became intense.

President James Madison's initial response to the growing tensions on the Southern frontier focused not on the Creek Nation, but on Spanish West Florida. Although the United States and Spain were not at war, Spain was an ally of Great Britain in Europe. Madison feared that the Spanish might either stir up the Southern American Indians against the United States or allow the British to use the West Florida ports of Mobile and Pensacola as bases from which to attack New Orleans. As few federal troops were available in the South, Secretary of War William Eustis asked Tennessee Governor William Blount to organize an

▲ John Armstrong, Jr. (1758–1843) had served in the American Revolutionary War, but was called back into service in 1812. The following year he was appointed secretary of war, although many in government opposed his elevation. (PD, via Wikimedia Commons)

Introduction

expedition against West Florida. Blount turned to his state militia commander, Major General Andrew Jackson, who quickly raised two thousand volunteers to reinforce New Orleans and to attack the Spanish.

On January 8, 1813, Jackson and his infantry departed Nashville, Tennessee, by boats down the Cumberland, Ohio, and Mississippi Rivers, while the Tennessee cavalry under the command of Colonel John Coffee rode down a trail known as the Natchez Trace. In February, the two columns converged at the capital of the Mississippi Territory, Washington, located six miles east of the Mississippi River town of Natchez. There, Jackson waited for further instructions concerning the movement on West Florida. By this time, however, the mood had changed in Congress and the administration shelved plans to invade West Florida. Informing Jackson that "the causes for embodying and marching to New Orleans the Corps under your command having ceased to exist," Secretary of War John Armstrong instructed the general to dismiss his volunteers from service, to turn over all equipment to U.S. Army authorities of the 7th Military District (which included Louisiana, Tennessee, and the Mississippi Territory), and to return to Tennessee.

When Jackson received Armstrong's letter in mid-March, he became enraged. He immediately fired off a reply informing him that he would disobey the order to turn in equipment and tents, which his men would need for their return journey. Since the U.S. government would not pay for rations on their return trip, Jackson arranged to procure them himself. He led his two thousand volunteers back to Tennessee on foot, giving up his own horse to carry the sick. Jackson's men dubbed him "Old Hickory" for the strength of character and fortitude he displayed.

Tensions along the frontier had not abated, however. In March, about the same time that Jackson started his trek back to Tennessee, Little Warrior, returning from another meeting with Tecumseh, murdered seven families at the mouth of the Ohio River. Moreover, Red Stick warriors began targeting Creeks friendly to the United States. The Madison administration reversed course yet again and ordered Major General James Wilkinson, who was based at New Orleans, to capture Mobile to stop British merchants located there from supplying the Red

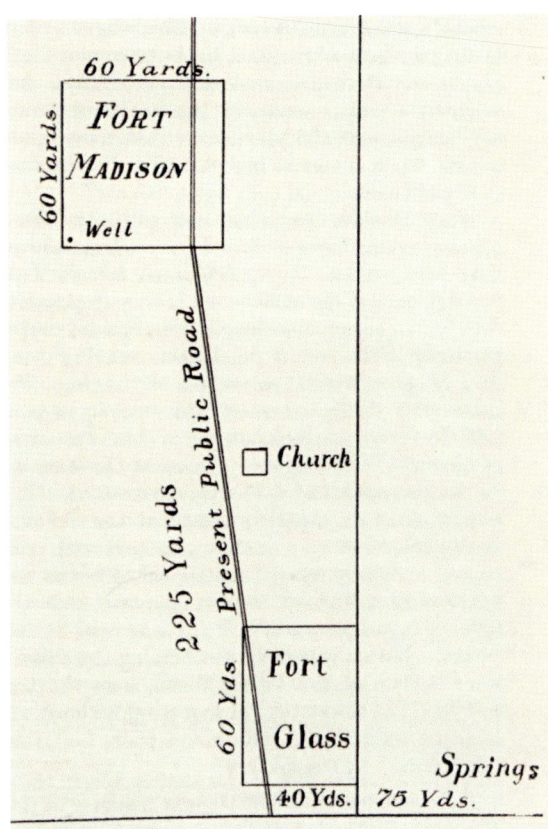

▼ A plan showing Fort Glass and Fort Madison in Clarke County, Alabama. Both were built as stockade forts during the Creek War, being heavily constructed of pine logs with blockhouses at the corners. (Henry S. Halbert/PD, via Wikimedia Commons)

17

The Creek War, 1813–14

Sticks with arms. Wilkinson complied, capturing Mobile without a fight in April. The fall of Mobile left Pensacola as the only source of weapons and ammunition available to the Red Sticks.

By June 1813, the Creek Nation was descending into civil war. Having won the backing of the majority of Creeks, the Red Sticks began gathering their forces near the confluence of the Coosa and Tallapoosa Rivers. There they executed several Creeks who had enforced the National Council's orders to bring perpetrators of violence to justice. Red Stick leaders announced that they intended to kill Hawkins and all headmen who supported the United States. They also planned to destroy both the national Creek capital of Tuckabatchee and the Lower Creek capital of Coweta.

◀ John Coffee. (Courtesy of Tennessee State Library and Archives)

In July, a Creek youth by the name of Latecau, who claimed to be a prophet, gathered a group of followers and traveled to the Creek town of Coosa. There, he invited all of the National Creek headmen who did not support the Red Stick movement to come and experience his religious powers. Many headmen from surrounding towns gathered to witness the proceedings. Latecau and other Red Stick believers began by performing the dances Tecumseh had taught them. During the dances, Latecau and his followers suddenly attacked the National Creek headmen, killing three. The other headmen fled Coosa, gathered together their warriors, and returned seeking revenge. The National Creeks managed to kill Latecau and eight of his followers at Coosa before moving on to Okfuskee and attacking more Red Stick followers. Fighting quickly escalated between the opposing factions as did the danger posed by the Red Sticks to whites traveling through or living near Creek lands. The governors of Georgia and Tennessee could not support the council since states could not send their militia into federal territory without the permission of the U.S. government.

Battle of Burnt Corn

With open warfare now all but assured, Red Stick leader Peter McQueen traveled to Pensacola with three hundred fifty Red Stick warriors to obtain arms and ammunition. At Pensacola, McQueen presented the Spanish governor, Mateo González Manrique, with a letter from a British general in Canada recommending that the Spanish supply the Red Sticks with weapons and ammunition. After hesitating at first, Manrique gave McQueen three hundred pounds of gunpowder and a proportionate amount of lead. While in Pensacola, the Creeks made statements that they intended to attack white settlements once they returned home. As verification of their statements, they spent several days engaged in dances and other ceremonies usually performed before going to war.

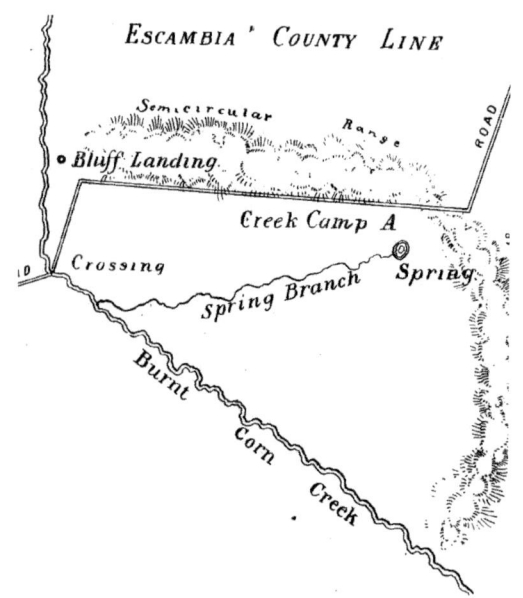

▼ A basic sketch map of the Burnt Corn battlefield, marking the location of the Creek camp and the hills that shielded the approach of Caller's troops as they advanced to contact. (Henry S. Halbert/PD, via Wikimedia Commons)

News of these developments quickly made its way to the settlers living in the Tensaw District of the Mississippi Territory, and the local militia commander, Colonel James Caller, mobilized his force. He decided to intercept McQueen and his party on their return trip from Pensacola before they could deliver the war supplies to the main Red Stick forces. Setting out on July 25, Caller took three companies of mounted militiamen armed with their own rifles and shotguns. Another company under the command of Captain Samuel Dale joined Caller. After crossing the Alabama River, Caller received additional reinforcements. He now commanded about one hundred eighty militiamen and National Creeks.

On the morning of July 27, Caller's scouts reported that the Red Sticks were camped a few miles ahead on the Pensacola Road in what is now northern Escambia County, Alabama. A council of war decided to divide

Profile:
Samuel Dale (1772–1841)

Samuel Dale is a quintessential American hero, his legend formed during the Creek War. He was born in 1772 in Rockbridge, Virginia, but his family moved many times, migrating to the Southwest until they came to rest in Greensborough, Georgia, where they worked a farm. It was a tough existence, made far tougher by the death of both his parents in 1792, which left him (aged 20) in charge of eight younger siblings.

Dale was a hardy frontiersman, and in 1793 joined a cavalry militia unit fighting Creeks, who regularly raided local settlements. Between 1796 and 1813, Dale ran a successful wagoning business, building up much experience of trading with the Native Americans, and also served as a guide to help federal forces map a road through Cherokee territory in northwest Georgia.

In the Creek War, Dale joined the militia and resumed the fight against the Creeks. His experience of Native American tactics, his intimate familiarity with the terrain, his resourcefulness and skill at arms, led to his being given the nickname the "Daniel Boone of Alabama." He fought at the battle of Burnt Corn Creek, where he was wounded, and in the famous clash on the Alabama River known as the "Canoe Fight." He then served with the troops of General Ferdinand Claiborne at Econochaca. In each of these clashes, and in many others, Dale distinguished himself. After the war, he held a variety of public offices in Alabama and Mississippi, serving on the legislatures of both states. He died on May 24, 1841, in Lauderdale County, Mississippi. The community of Daleville in Mississippi and Dale County in Alabama are named in his honor.

▶ The Canoe Fight on November 12, 1813, was a small but desperate clash between U.S. militia led by Captain Samuel Dale and Red Stick warriors. Dale is here seen boarding an enemy canoe and finishing the fight with his bayonet. (John McLenan/PD, via Wikimedia Commons)

The Creek War, 1813–14

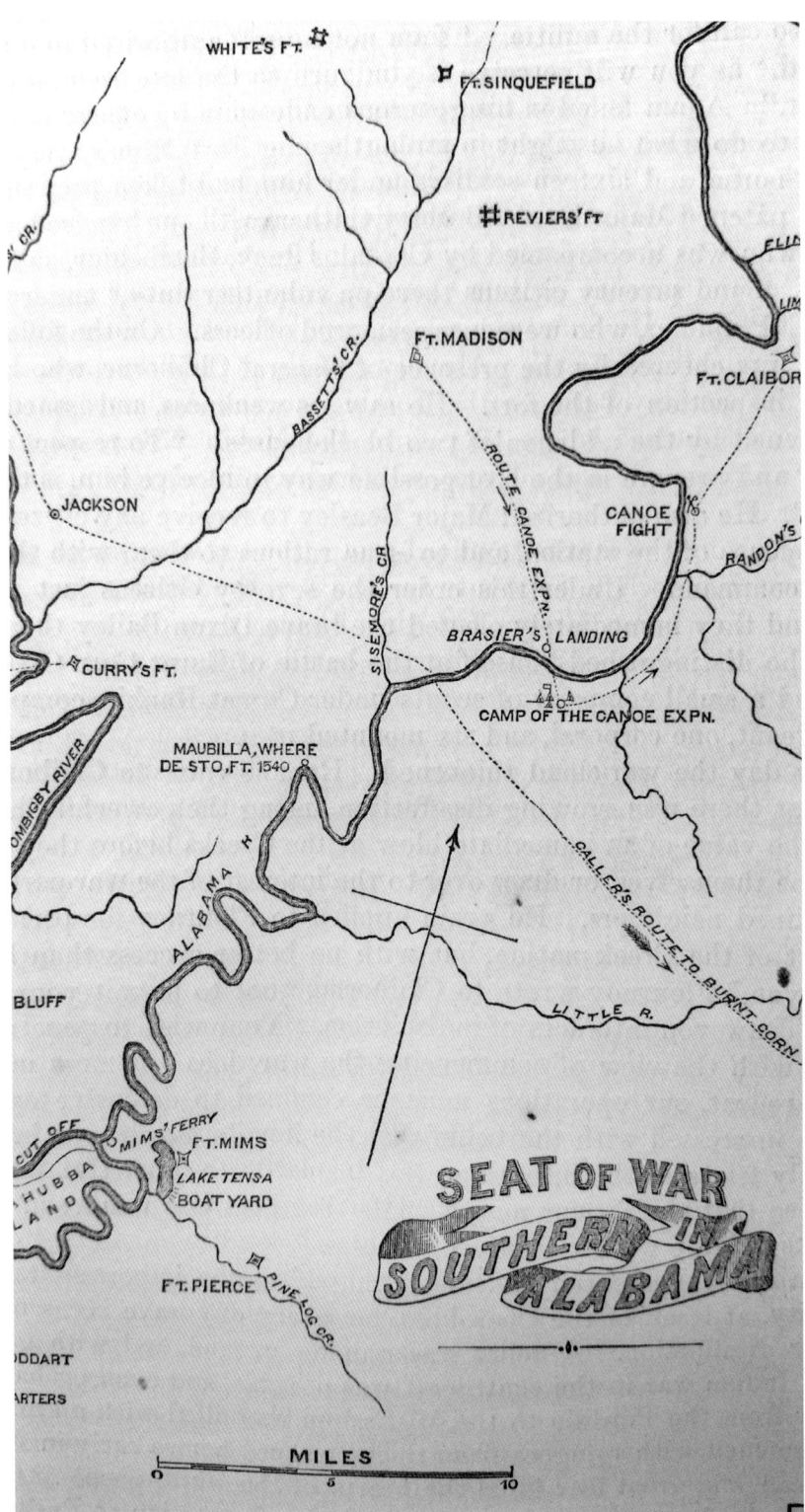

◀ A map showing southern Alabama during the Creek War. It marks the placement of several key forts, suggesting how their location and frequency was important for controlling territory, especially around waterways. It also shows, in the center, Caller's route of advance to Burnt Corn Creek. (Benson Lossing/PD, via Wikimedia Commons)

▲ The Native Americans made excellent tactical use of canoes during the Creek War. Made from birchbark, they had a shallow draft to negotiate most minor rivers and were also light enough for easy portage over land. Birchbark canoes at the Grand Portage National Monument historic encampment. (National Park Service)

the militiamen into three columns for the purpose of surrounding the Creek encampment, which was situated in a bend of Burnt Corn Creek. The hilly terrain hid the approach of Caller's troops, and the three-pronged assault surprised the Red Sticks and forced them to evacuate their camp. The militiamen then became occupied in leading off the American Indians' packhorses. After McQueen realized that the militia had stopped pursuing him, he regrouped his warriors and counterattacked, forcing the militiamen to flee. Both sides lost about a dozen men, but the militia escaped with most of the American Indians' supplies (see Map 2).

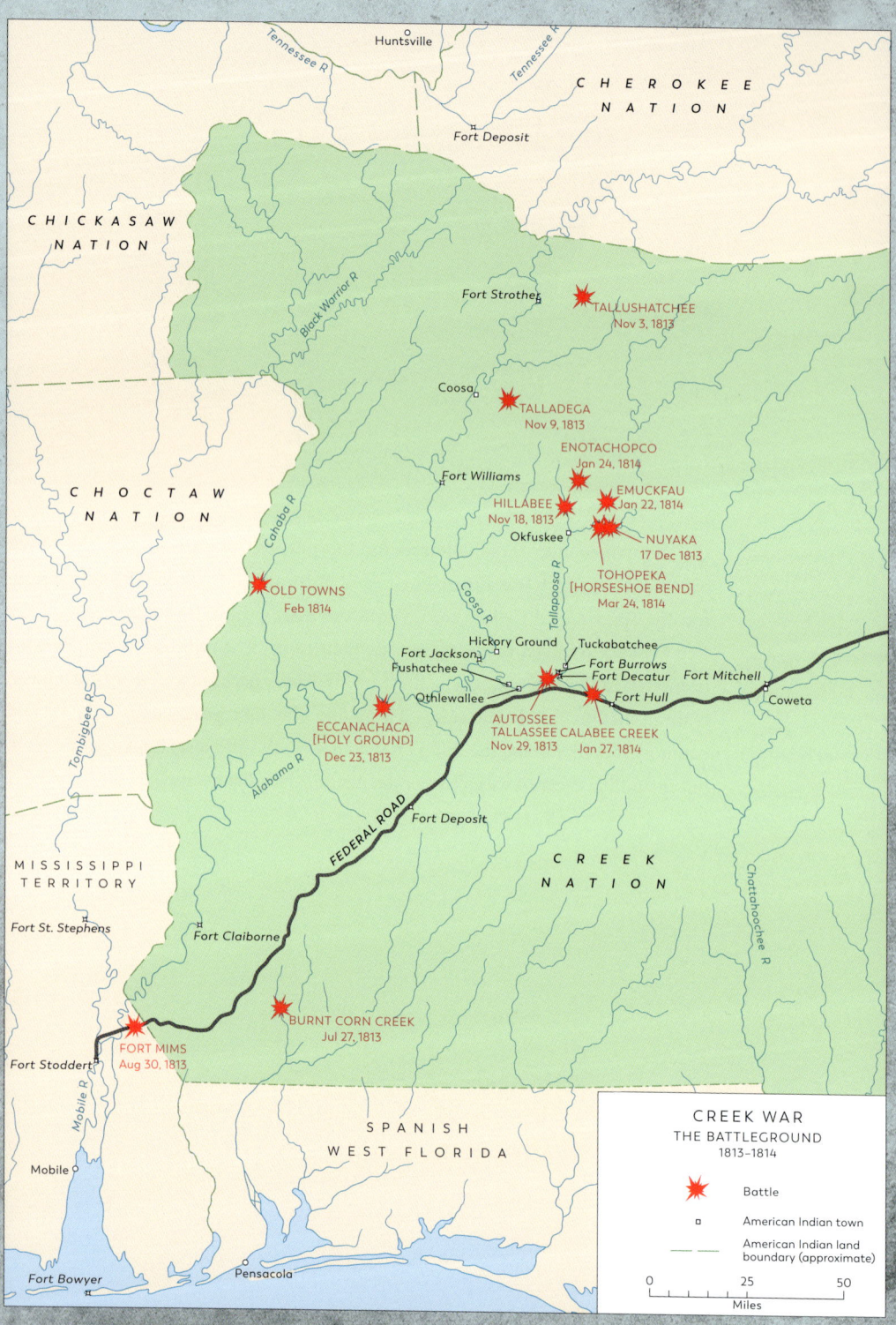
▲ Map 2

The Fort Mims Massacre

Immediately after the action at Burnt Corn Creek, the Red Sticks initiated a war against white settlers in the Tensaw District. The attacks caused many settlers to leave their remote homesteads for settlements near the confluence of the Tombigbee and Alabama Rivers. Scattered throughout the region were small stockade forts that generally consisted of a palisade erected around a settler's dwelling and other nearby structures. Each fort usually boasted at least one blockhouse in a corner to provide some cross-fire capability.

▼ A marker in Alabama clearly tells the bloody history of Fort Mims during the Creek War. As indicated, more than 500 people were killed in the massacre by the Red Sticks; they also destroyed the surrounding settlement, including killing thousands of cattle. (Don W. Robbins/PD, via Wikimedia Commons)

In response to the Creek attacks, Mississippi Territory authorities sent Brigadier General Ferdinand L. Claiborne to the Tensaw District with a large force of Mississippi Territory militia. Claiborne distributed his men so that every stockade fort would have at least some semblance of a garrison. He stationed 175 militiamen under the command of Major Daniel Beasley to one of the largest of the posts, Fort Mims, built around the house of local planter Samuel Mims about forty miles north of Mobile.

Fort Mims sheltered several hundred white and mixed-blood settlers along with the people they'd enslaved. The fort consisted of a compound of about one acre surrounded by a stockade. A lone blockhouse had been partially constructed on the southwest corner and some five hundred loopholes cut

25

The Creek War, 1813–14

in the stockade about three and a half feet off the ground. A building attached to the north palisade wall, referred to as "the bastion," had additional picketing around it. Although the fort sat on a small hill, potential attackers could approach close to the walls without being detected due to the nature of the surrounding terrain.

General Claiborne visited Fort Mims in early August. To his dismay, he found that the population of the settlement had become complacent. The general ordered Beasley to strengthen the palisade, to construct two additional blockhouses, and to send out regular patrols. By the end of August, Major Beasley still had not made the improvements ordered by General Claiborne and had even grown so careless as to allow the fort gates to be left open.

On August 30, about one thousand Red Stick warriors rushed the open eastern gate to Fort Mims in a noon assault. Before the garrison realized the danger, the warriors had control of three-fourths of the palisade loopholes and had struck down Major Beasley as he tried to close the gate. Captain Dixon Bailey assumed command of the garrison and attempted to mount a defense, but he could not shift troops sufficiently to regain portions of the fort. Instead, the garrison

▼ An engraving of the massacre at Fort Mims, depicting an attack on settlers and allied Creeks by the Red Sticks. (Alabama Department of Archives and History)

The Fort Mims Massacre

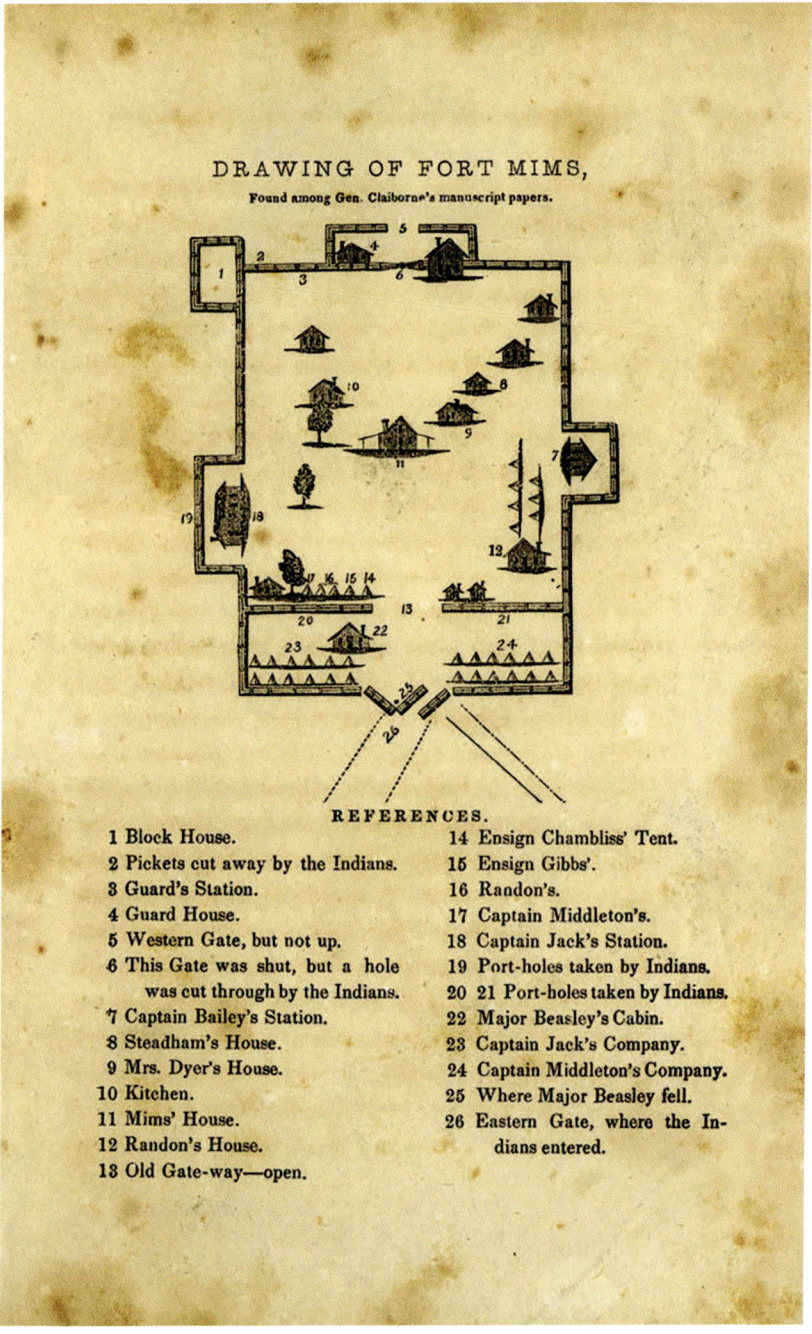

◀ Diagram of Fort Mims, allegedly from General Claiborne's papers. (Tennessee State Library and Archives/PD, via Wikimedia Commons)

divided into small groups and retreated toward the Mims house in the center, the unfinished blockhouse in the southwest corner, and the bastion on the north wall. Eventually, the warriors overran the blockhouse but could not budge the defenders from the Mims house and the bastion. The defenders continued to

The Creek War, 1813–14

fight off attacks on the remaining two enclaves until late afternoon when the Creeks withdrew. During this lull, the garrison regrouped and prepared as best it could for a renewed assault, which came almost immediately.

During the second assault, the Red Sticks shot flaming arrows into the two remaining defensive positions. These had the desired effect of flushing out the defenders of the Mims house into the open where Red Sticks shot them down. With most of the fort now in flames and only a few whites left alive, Captain Bailey directed the survivors to escape as best they could. The battle was over by 1700. The warriors took no prisoners, killing the inhabitants without mercy.

▲ A view inside the reconstructed Fort Mims, looking towards the west wall, 2006. (Don W. Robbins, via Wikimedia Commons)

▼ Fort Hawkins, today in Georgia, is typical of the fortifications built by the U.S. military during the early 19th century. This photograph shows inside the upper level of the reconstructed southeastern blockhouse. (PD, via Wikimedia Commons)

Tennessee and Andrew Jackson

Before the attack on Fort Mims, Benjamin Hawkins had assured Secretary of War Armstrong that the Red Stick hostilities could be dealt with by the National Council and those Creeks who supported it. Tennessee's Governor Blount, however, had suggested in June 1812 that the best means of preventing further Red Stick hostilities might be to mount a military expedition into Creek territory. The continued attacks by Red Stick warriors throughout the summer also made the secretary realize that force might be necessary. He wrote to Georgia Governor David B. Mitchell on July 13, 1813 requesting that he organize an army of fifteen hundred militiamen for operations in the Creek territory.

Armstrong delineated a plan for the Georgia militia to cooperate with Tennessee forces and the 3d U.S. Infantry Regiment stationed at Mobile. He sent a similar letter to Governor Blount. This three-pronged pincer movement from the north, east, and southwest would, the secretary hoped, overwhelm the Red Sticks. Armstrong asked the governors to give him a timeline of when they could have their forces ready to take the field so that he could coordinate their movements with those of the 3d Infantry.

Like Mitchell, Blount planned to raise fifteen hundred militia for the coming campaign. Naturally, he turned to the commander of Tennessee's militia, General Jackson, to lead the foray. Friends of Jackson in Washington, D.C., had already informed him of the government's decision to send military forces into Creek territory. Before Blount could advise Jackson, the general wrote to the governor offering suggestions as to Tennessee's role in the pending conflict. He suggested that the need to guard supply lines and the possible involvement of the British and Spanish meant that Tennessee should provide three thousand to five thousand

The Creek War, 1813–14

militia. He recommended that the manpower be drawn evenly from the eastern and western militia districts of the state.

When news of the Fort Mims disaster reached Nashville on September 18, 1813, Jackson was bedridden with wounds received from a recent duel. He nevertheless assured Blount and the town's leading citizens that he would personally lead the expedition into the Creek lands. Heeding Jackson's advice, Blount directed the general to raise twenty-five hundred militia from the western part of the state and a like number from the eastern part. The next day, Jackson issued orders calling out the state militia. Knowing that assembling men from around the state would require time, he ordered the immediate formation of a cavalry regiment and sent it south to the Creek frontier. He entrusted the command of the mounted unit to Colonel Coffee, hoping that the horsemen would be able to stabilize the frontier until he arrived with the main army. Jackson directed Coffee to move south toward Huntsville in what is now the state of Alabama. Jackson personally planned to lead the western militia then gathering at Fayetteville, Tennessee, eighty miles south of Nashville. The eastern militia gathered at Knoxville, Tennessee, under the command of Major General John A. Cocke.

▼ A classic Native American war bonnet, currently on display in the Pacific Grove Museum of Natural History, Pacific Grove, California. Each eagle feather denotes an act of leadership or bravery, and only high-status individuals would be eligible to wear the headdress. (Daderot/ CC0 1.0, via Wikimedia Commons)

Tennessee and Andrew Jackson

Jackson arrived at the Fayetteville militia camp on October 7, 1813. Friendly Cherokee warriors also joined his assembling army. Soon after his arrival, he received word from Coffee that Red Stick warriors were moving northward toward the Tennessee River. The colonel feared that his regiment of five hundred mounted militiamen might be overwhelmed if not immediately supported. On October 11, Jackson and his army reached Huntsville, having traveled over thirty miles in ten hours. The alarm proved to be false, but Jackson now had his army close to the Creek towns.

After several days at Huntsville, Jackson sent Coffee's cavalry along the upper reaches of the Black Warrior River to raid Red Stick towns located in that region. Meanwhile, he moved the infantry up the Tennessee River to establish a new supply base, Fort Deposit, in the northern part of the Mississippi Territory. He intended to march south down the Coosa River to the important Creek town of Hickory Ground, located near the junction of the Coosa and Tallapoosa Rivers, hopefully in coordination with Brigadier General John Floyd's Georgians supposedly advancing from the east. Moving from Fort Deposit, Jackson and his Tennesseans had to negotiate the southern end of the Appalachian Mountains,

▼ A Native American war shirt. Note the strands of human hair dangling from around the collar; these would indicate the wearer's power over his enemies and his bravery in battle. (CC0, Art Institute of Chicago)

building a road as they went so that supply wagons could follow them. Once over the mountains, Jackson reached the Coosa River at the Ten Islands on November 1. There, he had Fort Strother constructed as a forward supply point.

In the meantime, General Cocke and his army of East Tennessee militia made their way down the Tennessee River, to present-day Chattanooga, then overland through northwest Georgia. As commander of Tennessee's militia, Jackson clearly intended Cocke to join his own forces, but Cocke held the same rank in the state militia and did not feel obligated to subordinate himself to Jackson's authority. He considered Jackson a political rival and wanted any victories won by the East Tennessee forces attributed to himself, and not Jackson.

While his men built Fort Strother, Jackson learned of a large Red Stick force located at the Creek town of Tallushatchee, some fifteen miles distant. He ordered Coffee to attack the town with about one thousand mounted militia. Coffee surrounded the village on November 3, and then sent two companies to lure the warriors out of their position. The Red Sticks took the bait and rushed out of the town and into the ring of Tennessee militia. The subsequent militia attack forced the Red Stick warriors back into the town as the dragoons tightened the circle. After the battle the horsemen set fire to the buildings. Red Stick losses amounted to 186 warriors killed and some 80 women and children captured, while Coffee sustained fewer than 50 casualties.

After Coffee's victory at Tallushatchee, many nearby Creek towns pledged their loyalty to the United States. About one hundred loyal Creeks sought

▲ The now-distant battles of American history have endured in the American memory. Here is a marker erected by children of Clark County in 1931 to remember the twelve women and children killed at Fort Sinquefield in the "Kimbell-James Massacre" of September 1, 1813. (Jeffrey Reed/CC BY-SA 3.0, via Wikimedia Commons)

Tennessee and Andrew Jackson

refuge at Fort Leslie near the Creek town of Talladega in what is now the state of Alabama. About one thousand Red Sticks led by William Weatherford surrounded Fort Leslie, stating that he would kill all inside unless the occupants joined him in warring against the United States. A Creek American Indian from the fort managed to elude the besiegers and carry word of the situation to Jackson at Fort Strother.

Although low on food and supplies, Jackson thought that a victory at Talladega might end the war. Learning that a contingent of East Tennessee militia under Brigadier General James White was approaching, Jackson ordered White to hasten to Fort Strother and secure the post. He then left a small guard and the wounded from the Tallushatchee fight behind and immediately marched to Talladega, about twenty miles farther south, with twelve hundred infantry and eight hundred cavalry. On the night of November 8, a courier from Fort Strother arrived with a letter from White informing Jackson that his East Tennessee militia would not be arriving at Fort Strother because General Cocke had ordered his troops back to their main camp in western Georgia. Undeterred, Jackson continued with his offensive. On November 9, his two thousand Tennesseans approached Talladega. Through an error, his force failed to encircle the town as Jackson had intended. Weatherford escaped with about seven hundred warriors, leaving three hundred men to perish in a furious battle when Jackson's troops

▼ A marker placed by the Alabama Anthropological Society in 1931 indicates the site of Fort Decatur, which lay on the banks of the Tallapoosa River. Rather than a wooden stockage fortification, Fort Decatur was of earthen construction. (Rivers Langley; SaveRivers/CC BY-SA 4.0)

The Creek War, 1813–14

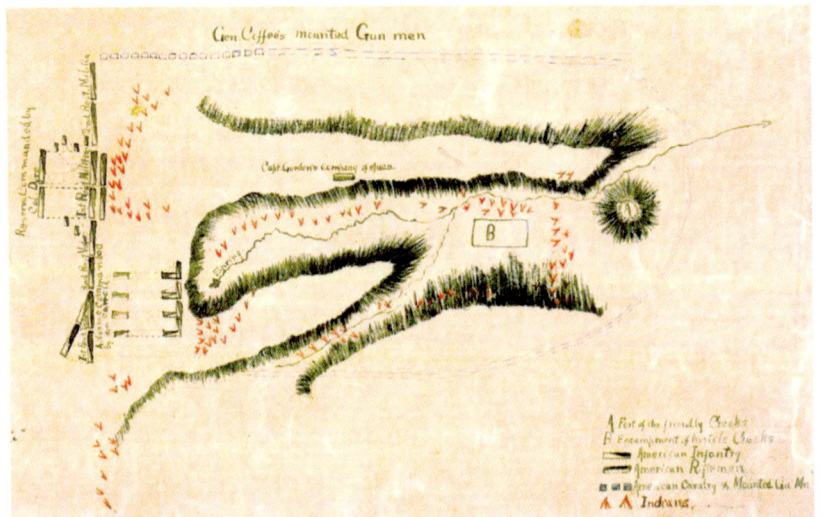

▲ An artwork from 1852 depicts "Gen. Coffee's attack on the Indians," the victory at Tallushatchee. The artist also seems to convey the lack of mercy shown to the Native American warriors and families. (PD, via Wikimedia Commons)

attacked. Jackson's army sustained about one hundred casualties. The general complained afterward that "had we had provisions, this stroke by following it up would have put an end to the war."

◀ Hand-drawn sketch of the battle of Talladega, 1813. (Wikimedia Commons/Alabama Department of Archives and History)

Eyewitness:
The battle of Tallushatchee

The following eyewitness account of the battle of Tallushatchee comes from the extensive journal of Richard Keith Call, who served as a young lieutenant during the Creek War and later went on to be appointed twice as the territorial governor of Florida. His testimony gives a sense of the drama and violence of the attack; later parts of his testimony reflect on the dreadful slaughter and cruelty to the Native Americans by merciless U.S. troops. The original spellings are here retained:

> The next day we entered the enemy's country, all on Tiptoes of expectation of adventure. This night General Coffee with his brigade was detached to cross the Coosey and attack the town of Tallashstchee, situated near the eastern Bank of that river. The surprise was complete, his success eminent. Without discovery the town was entirely surrounded early in the morning. So soon as our men were seen on one flank, the Indian drum sounded the alarm, which was answered by the wild war whoop of one hundred and eighty warriors, who sprang to their arms, and rushed with impetuous valour to the only point they then knew to be assailed. On they came, yelling like demons, to the charge. The field being open—they were freely exposed—but they were bravely met, and the well aimed rifles of the gallant Tennesseans caused many to fall, and the remainder to fly back to the town where they were followed, the lines closing up on them. A desperate fight ensued, and continued with terrible slaughter until the last warrior fell, leaving none but women and children—and many of them were slain unavoidably—indeed many of the women fought themselves bravely from the houses of the village using the bow and arrow with great effect—but being overcome they were led in triumph to General Jackson's camp.

The battles at Tallushatchee and Talladega significantly diminished Red Stick strength, and by rescuing friendly Creeks at Talladega, Jackson further cemented the relationship between National Council Creeks and the United States. Impressed by American power, the Creeks of the Hillabee towns, located in the northern Creek territory, pledged not to war any further against the United States. In return, General Jackson promised not to attack their towns.

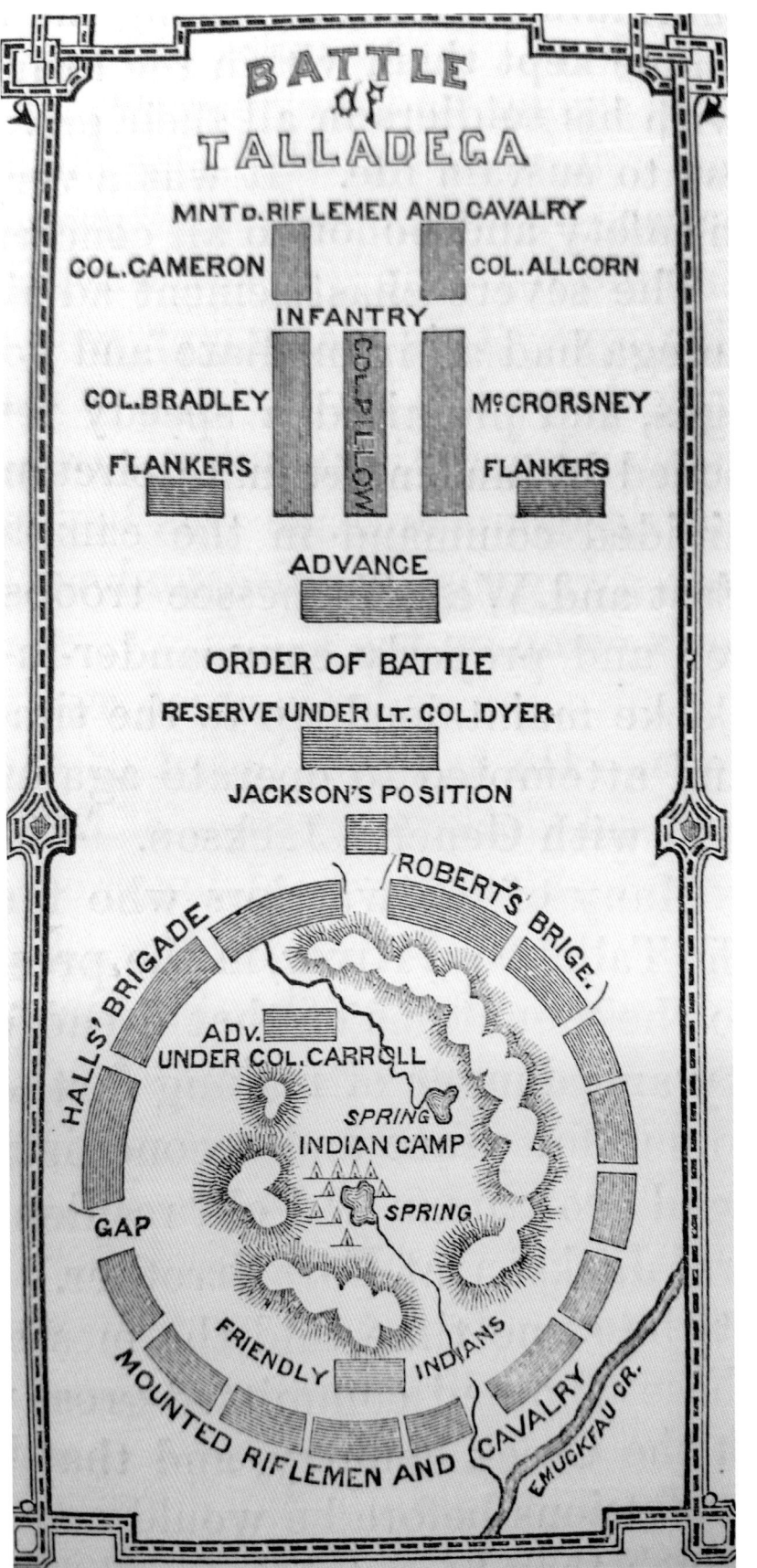

◀ A particularly orderly plan of the battle of Talladega. The battle resulted in a disproportionate number of Native American dead compared to American casualties. (Benson Lossing/PD, via Wikimedia Commons)

Profile:
Traditional Native American weapons

The Native Americans had a traditional arsenal that separated into projectile, impact, or edged categories. The principal projectile weapons were the composite bow, which was short enough for use from horseback as well as dismounted, and the spear, the latter given additional range in some tribes by the *atlatl* spear-throwing device (a hooked piece of wood designed to impart extra leverage to the throw). Well-trained warriors could also throw the war hatchet (a type of battleaxe) or tomahawk, although these were also used for hand-held fighting. (The standard range of a thrown tomahawk was around twelve feet, but talented individuals could hit targets out to thirty feet.) The Native Americans also relied upon a variety of clubs for close-in fighting. The three main types were: 1) the stone club, built from a wooden haft with a heavy stone lashed on one end as the impact point; 2) solid wooden clubs, typically carved from hardwoods such as oak, elm, maple, hickory, or cherry, with a slender handle but swelling out to a bulbous or pointed head; 3) the gunstock war club, a flat club carved in a general profile resembling, deliberately, the woodwork of a musket. This was held and swung from the narrow end, and blades were occasionally fitted to the striking edge. The Native Americans also carried daggers. For most of their history, the indigenous people of North America used shaped flint or obsidian to form the blades, but interactions with the settlers from the 16th century brought increasing adoption of iron and then steel blades, either through purchase or by adopting Western steel-making practices on a small scale.

▼ A Native American ball-headed club, dating back to the early 1800s. Note how the ball is gripped by a form of mouth; this was meant to imbue the weapon and its handler with animal-like powers. (Andrew R. and Martha Holden Jennings Fund/ CC0 1.0, via Wikimedia Commons)

The Creek War, 1813–14

Unfortunately, General Cocke knew nothing of these arrangements. On November 10, he directed General White with his mounted East Tennessee militia and some three hundred Cherokee warriors to attack the Hillabee towns. Since the Creeks did not expect an attack, they were completely defenseless when White attacked on November 18. In fact, when White attacked at first light, many residents came out to greet the Tennesseans and Cherokees. The towns contained many warriors wounded from the battles at Tallushatchee and Talladega as well as women and children. White took the women and children prisoners and reported killing sixty-nine Creek warriors. His own command sustained no casualties. When Jackson heard of the attack he became furious. He viewed the slaughter as evidence of Cocke's insubordination. The surviving Hillabees believed they had been double-crossed by Jackson and henceforth pledged to war against the United States.

His string of victories notwithstanding, Jackson struggled to keep a respectable military force assembled. Upon his return to Fort Strother after Talladega, he found that supplies had not reached that post from Fort Deposit as intended. The men grumbled about the lack of supplies and threatened to leave camp. Jackson issued a proclamation imploring the militiamen to remain at Fort Strother, stating that the campaign would end thirty days after sufficient supplies had arrived. Assuming the supply train from Fort Deposit would arrive momentarily, he promised his troops that if provisions did

▶ A beautifully crafted 19th-century pipe tomahawk. These weapon/pipe combinations were used both in warfighting and for smoking during trade and diplomatic negotiations with the settlers. (Historical Museum of Bern/CC BY-SA 2.0 FR, via Wikimedia Commons)

not arrive in two days, he would personally lead them back to the Tennessee River.

When no supply train arrived, Jackson led his troops northward toward Fort Deposit on November 17, where he knew there would be provisions. The column had only marched about twelve miles when it met a supply column from Fort Deposit consisting of nine wagons carrying flour and one hundred fifty head of cattle. Jackson's troops halted and gorged on the supplies.

After the hungry troops had eaten, Jackson ordered the column back to Fort Strother, but some militia units decided to continue their march home. Jackson and his staff blocked the road and the troops, in "a turbulent and mutinous disposition," backed down. After having to stop a second mass desertion, this time with loaded muskets, Jackson rode to Fort Deposit, accompanied by Coffee and his mounted troops, to investigate the supply situation. At Fort Deposit, Jackson sent Coffee northward to the Huntsville area so he could obtain remounts and forage his horses in greener pastures. He also wrote to Major General Thomas Flournoy, the commander of the 7th Military District that included the Mississippi Territory, asking for supplies and reinforcements.

◄ Made from smoke-dried deerskin and porcupine quills, this Native American dagger case shows exquisite levels of craftsmanship. By the 19th century, the traditional stone, bone, or obsidian blades of Native American knives had largely been replaced by iron or steel. (Daderot/CC0 1.0, via Wikimedia Commons)

The Georgia Militia and the Offensive from the East

During the summer of 1813, Governor Mitchell appointed Brigadier General John Floyd to lead Georgia's contribution to war against the Red Sticks. Floyd established his headquarters at the state capital at Milledgeville to supervise logistical preparations and the assembling of the troops. Like Jackson, supply shortages bedeviled the Georgian leader. He quickly discovered that Major General Thomas Pinckney, the commander of the 6th Military District that included Georgia, had no tents or camp equipment for his use. Additionally, any rations provided to the army could only be transported as far as the western limit of the state. Beyond that, Floyd would have to arrange wagons, horses, and drivers.

As summer faded into fall, Georgia officials struggled to feed Floyd's growing army, and to accumulate the thirty days' supply of food stocks Floyd deemed necessary to sustain the campaign once it began. With so many men assembled in closely confined camps, sanitation became an issue and disease broke out.

With his force only partially trained and the supply problem still not overcome, Floyd moved out of Milledgeville on October 29. He carried with him only a twenty days' supply of flour and three days of beef for his army, but anticipated being overtaken by additional supply trains. On November 3, the day Coffee's mounted Tennesseans defeated the Red Sticks at Tallushatchee, Floyd arrived at Fort Lawrence on the Federal Road west of the Flint River, roughly twenty miles from Macon, Georgia. He intended to use this post as the major supply point for his campaign and as the final staging area for his forces. Within two weeks, he had accumulated enough supplies for twenty days and began marching toward

The Georgia Militia and the Offensive from the East

Coweta on the Chattahoochee River that was under siege by the Red Sticks. He had almost fifteen hundred men and two cannon with him, having left over two hundred fifty sick men at Fort Lawrence. By the time Floyd's column reached the town, however, the Red Sticks had learned of his approach and had abandoned the siege.

After picking up some interpreters from Benjamin Hawkins, the Georgians crossed the Chattahoochee River on November 24, 1813. There, Floyd established Fort Mitchell in what is now Alabama to act as a forward supply center. At this point, Floyd decided to attack the Red Stick town of Autossee, situated along the Tallapoosa River about sixty miles to the west. Without waiting for Fort Mitchell to be completed, he led his army westward and arrived within eight miles of Autossee late in the day of November 28. Curiously, the Red Sticks did not attack. Floyd rousted his army in the middle of the night and arrived outside the town around daybreak on the twenty-ninth. He wanted to surround the town so that no warriors could escape, but on surveying the area, he discovered that another settlement, Tallassee, lay contiguous to Autossee. Together, the villages were too large for him to encircle. He therefore divided his forces to attack the two

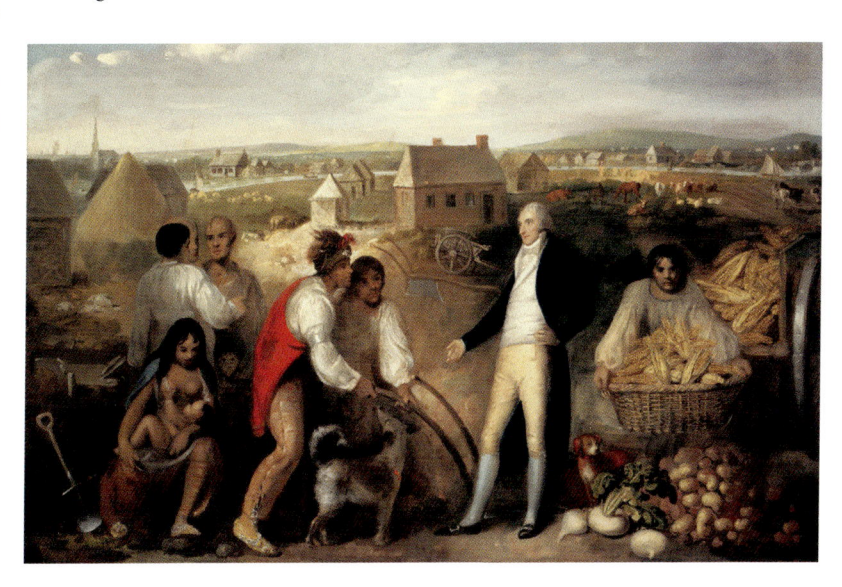

▲ A portrait of Thomas Pinckney, governor of South Carolina between 1787 and 1789 and a major general in the War of 1812, during which he commanded the Southern Division of the U.S. Army. He saw no combat, but took charge of developing coastal defenses. (National Portrait Gallery)

▶ A munificent vision of interaction between the Native Americans and the U.S. government—Benjamin Hawkins instructs Creeks on his plantation how to use a plow. (PD, via Wikimedia Commons)

The Creek War, 1813–14

towns simultaneously. After two to three hours of exchanging small arms fire, neither side had gained a decided advantage. Floyd then employed his two field pieces with telling effect. After the artillery had made its impression, he ordered a bayonet attack that finally cleared the towns. The chiefs of both Autossee and Tallassee perished in the combat along with about two hundred others, but many other warriors escaped. The Georgia casualties amounted to over sixty, including Floyd, who retained command despite a serious wound in the knee.

Floyd allowed his Creek allies to plunder the villages before putting them to the torch. Like Jackson, the victorious Georgian did not have the resources to maintain a sustained campaign, and he ordered his army to withdraw. A few Red Stick warriors attacked his rear guard, but the Georgians quickly dispersed them. Once back at Fort Mitchell, Floyd set about tending to the wounded and stockpiling supplies for a second campaign.

While General Floyd and the other wounded Georgians recuperated, General Pinckney ordered Major General David Adams with his independent command of five hundred Georgia militiamen to keep the Red Sticks on the defensive and disrupt their food supplies. Adams led his men westward toward the Tallapoosa River, and on December 17 he struck the town of Nuyaka. The Georgians found the place deserted. Adams surmised correctly that the Red Sticks had learned of his approach and had fled rather than offer battle. After burning the town, Adams led his troops back to Georgia.

▼ This vivid artwork, produced in 1825, depicts "Georgia Militia under Gen. Floyd, attacking the Creek Indians at Autossee—Nov 29, 1813'." Note how the Creeks are armed with a mixture of bows and firearms. (JWB/PD, via Wikimedia Commons)

Native American tactics

In warfare, Native American tactics during the 18th and 19th centuries were a matter of continuity and change. The continuity lay in the deep-seated traditionalism inherent in their fighting methods, embedded into their culture over centuries. The changes were brought about by technology, particularly the spreading adoption of firearms, plus responses and countermeasures to the tactics of U.S. militia and federal forces.

For centuries, raiding was the chief tactic of Native American warriors, especially among the woodland American Indians of the eastern and northern parts of North America. Raids were both symbolic and martial events. After conducting a variety of sacred pre-fight rituals, a group of raiders would move covertly to positions overlooking an enemy camp or village, then make a frenzied attack at dawn, killing and (if possible) scalping enemy warriors and taking captives, the latter for either adoption, enslavement, or torture. Casualties in these clashes could be relatively low; the very survival of hunter-gatherer societies would be at risk from conflicts involving mass casualties, although occasionally there would be significant numbers of dead or wounded. Tactically, the focus was on a stealthy approach, a fast-paced attack (often firing on the move), and close-quarters combat, in which the spirit and fighting skills of the individual warrior would be uppermost.

The fight between the Native Americans and the European settlers was different, however. Settler expansion, aided by large militias and, later, federal troops, not only brought the Native Americans into contact with far more destructive forms of warfare, but also threatened the very territories in which they existed. The signal change this brought about was one of scale. Threatened tribes would expand raids to involve as many warriors as possible, hundreds or even thousands strong, often by forming confederacies. These great armies could, and did, win major battles against the settler forces, who were often overwhelmed by the fluidity of their enemy's movement and the persistence and speed of the attack. It took many decades for the settlers to adjust to the Native American tactics, but adjust they did. Native American forces learned the hard way about how many lives would be lost attacking a tightly defended, well-armed American position, and how terribly they could be overwhelmed by mass formations of disciplined infantry and cavalry using coordinated maneuver tactics. Ultimately, the traditional Native American ways of war could not adapt to the scale or firepower of settler armies, nor the strategies of American policy-makers.

The Mississippi Militia

The third thrust into Creek lands by American forces in the fall of 1813 originated in the southern part of the Mississippi Territory. In response to a request from Jackson, General Flournoy ordered General Claiborne to advance northward with his Mississippi militia up the Alabama River. Claiborne advanced with about two hundred fifty men under Colonel Joseph Carson, another one hundred fifty Mississippi militia under Major Benjamin Smoot, one hundred fifty mounted Mississippi militia under Major Cassels, and one hundred fifty Choctaw warriors under Pushmataha—in all about seven hundred men.

In mid-November, Claiborne built a fort on the Alabama River at Weatherford's Bluff, situated about halfway between present-day Montgomery and Mobile, Alabama. While gathering supplies at the new post, named Fort Claiborne, he also conducted operations against Red Stick communications with the Spanish at Pensacola. In late November, about fifty Choctaw warriors under Chief Pushmataha ambushed a Red Stick force at the old Burnt Corn Creek battleground.

On November 28, the same day Floyd camped near Autossee, Colonel Gilbert C. Russell arrived at Fort Claiborne from Mobile with four hundred regulars of the 3d Infantry. Russell and Claiborne devised a strategy that called for a quick strike deep into Red Stick territory. Their primary target was the most important Red Stick town, Eccanachaca, or the Holy Ground, located on a bluff on the Alabama River ten miles east of present-day Montgomery. A group of militia officers drafted a petition against the intended offensive, citing the approaching expiration of their enlistments, supply shortages, wintry weather, and the lack of warm clothing. Not wanting to be accused of mutiny, however, the officers

▶ *Pushmataha*, by John William Gear from a painting by Charles Bird King. (National Portrait Gallery, Smithsonian Institution)

concluded their remonstrance with an affirmation that they would continue to serve if Claiborne decided to conduct the offensive.

Claiborne indeed opted to attack Eccanachaca, and he marched his army eighty miles northward to establish another depot he dubbed Fort Deposit (not to be confused with the post of that name established by Jackson on the Tennessee River). He left his supply train and all unnecessary baggage there and continued his march to the vicinity of Eccanachaca. Six days after Adams' Georgians had attacked Nuyaka, Claiborne's men began their final march on Eccanachaca. Around 1100 on December 23, Claiborne halted some two miles from the village and issued his last orders. Choctaw scouts advised him that only about six hundred Creeks were in the village. At that point, Claiborne thought he could completely encircle the town and made his dispositions accordingly. He divided his force into three columns. He placed the 3d Infantry and the reserve in the center under his personal command, positioned the Mississippi militia led by Colonel Carson on the right, and posted a battalion of militia under Major

The Creek War, 1813–14

◀ This photograph is of the modern Holy Ground Battlefield Park in White Hall, Alabama. Note the density of trees bordering the river, which would have presented difficult terrain for the movement of large-scale forces in formation. (Rivers Langley; SaveRivers/CC BY-SA 3.0, via Wikimedia Commons)

Smoot with Pushmataha's Choctaw warriors on the left. He directed the mounted militia to place itself between the town and the Tallapoosa River, while Carson circled around to attack the town from the north.

Carson encountered difficult terrain that prevented him from executing the envelopment maneuver. When his troops finally emerged northeast of Eccanachaca, Red Sticks lying in defilade ambushed them. Undeterred, the Mississippi militia absorbed the volleys and continued with their attack. About half an hour later the Red Sticks withdrew.

By this time, the central column under Claiborne and the left column under Smoot and Pushmataha had engaged the Red Sticks at Eccanachaca. As

Claiborne's militiamen and the 3d Infantry began to push the enemy warriors from the south, Smoot and Pushmataha also pressed their attack from the west and north. The three-sided attack proved too much for the Red Stick warriors who gradually fell back into a smaller circle of defense. After a while the Red Stick warriors lost all cohesion. Those who had been in the town began to flee. Some crossed the Alabama River, while others escaped into the marshland.

Claiborne allowed Pushmataha and his Choctaw warriors to pillage the town, while his soldiers searched for hidden inhabitants. He then burned the community. His soldiers had killed thirty-three Red Stick warriors while sustaining only one killed and twenty wounded. Though not as complete a victory as Claiborne had hoped, the engagement at the Holy Ground boosted the morale of his men. It also showed the Red Sticks that they could be attacked in remote places that they had presumed to be immune from assault.

The army spent the night at Eccanachaca and the next day began a sweep through the area destroying everything that could aid the Red Sticks. Claiborne headed to the plantation of Red Stick leader William Weatherford. Claiborne discovered a letter of Weatherford's that proved the complicity of the Spanish in supplying arms, ammunition, and other provisions to the Red Sticks. He also found a letter from the Spanish governor of Pensacola congratulating Weatherford for the destruction of Fort Mims and advising against a contemplated Red Stick attack on Mobile.

▼ A late 19th-century picture of Native American life. The wars between the Native Americans and the settlers were often brutal because both sides blurred the lines between civilian and combatant, leading to some atrocious massacres. (Metropolitan Museum of Art; Gift of Mrs. Robert Ingersoll Aitken, 1951)

The Creek War, 1813–14

After spending a cold, miserable Christmas huddled around campfires in a drenching rain with nothing to eat but parched corn, the Mississippians and Choctaws began their return march to Fort Claiborne. Most of the enlistments of his militiamen had already expired, but the men had stayed in the field out of devotion to Claiborne. Once back at the fort, the now exhausted militiamen eagerly returned to their homes. The Choctaws under Pushmataha also departed, as did Claiborne, who received permission to return home due to illness. This left Colonel Russell with his regulars of the 3d Infantry and a company of Mississippi militia whose enlistments had not yet expired as the only cohesive American force in the Tensaw District. Refusing to remain idle, Russell dispatched a force of Chickasaws under the command of John McKee to raid Red Stick towns located along the Black Warrior River north of Fort Claiborne. McKee advanced as far as present-day Tuscaloosa, but he found all the towns abandoned and returned to Fort Claiborne.

▲ The grave of William Weatherford, aka Red Eagle, who led the attack on Fort Mims in August 1813. To the left of this grave, out of shot, is the grave of his mother, Sehoy Tate Weatherford. (Don W. Robbins/PD, via Wikimedia Commons)

Jackson and the Tennessee Volunteers

While Generals Floyd and Claiborne harried the Red Sticks from the east and south, respectively, during the closing weeks of 1813, supply shortages had kept General Jackson idle in the north. After spending several weeks at Fort Deposit wrestling with logistical matters, Jackson returned to Fort Strother in early December confident that he and Governor Blount had finally alleviated the army's supply problems.

Eager to resume the offensive, to his dismay Jackson found the army in a mutinous mood, with many militiamen asserting that their enlistments would expire on December 10. Fearing that he would lose most of his men, Jackson ordered

▶ *Jackson Quelling the Mutiny.* (Library of Congress)

Profile:
Wooden fortifications

The U.S. Army of the 18th and 19th centuries was adept at erecting wooden forts in contested areas. There were all manner of these structures, ingenious in design and adaptive in layout. The simplest might consist of little more than a circular outer palisade surrounding living quarters for a company of men, while the most advanced would cover several acres and accommodate hundreds of troops.

The wooden forts were temporary or semi-permanent defenses for a fixed number of men, built in a location where timber was plentiful in the natural surroundings. A common type of structure was a stockade fort, in which an outer wall was constructed from vertical tree trunks, sharpened at one end and driven into the floor of a ditch, the ditch being back-filled and the logs lashed together to hold the structure upright. To strengthen the defendability of the outer wall, the troops might also dig an outer ditch and heap the earth up against the logs, and/or pile up thick brushwood to confound attackers attempting to close up to the wall. The log frontage would also feature loopholes through which the troops could fire. A substantial wooden fort would include bastioned corners: each corner would feature an angled wooden structure presenting two faces, to increase the angles of fire along and out from the wall. Blockhouses—fully enclosed four-sided and roofed buildings—might also be set at the corners or within the interior of the fort, the upper floor acting as a protected, elevated platform for 360-degree fire from muskets and even light cannon.

▲ At Fort Mitchell Historic Park, Alabama, there is a reconstruction of the 1813 stockade fort, seen here. The original was built during the Creek War as a military outpost, and was rebuilt and garrisoned intermittently during the remainder of the 19th century. (dofftoubab/CC BY-SA 3.0, via Wikimedia Commons)

General Cocke to bring his East Tennessee militia to Fort Strother and asked Blount to raise more militia. He also warned Coffee, whose mounted militiamen were recuperating near Huntsville, to be prepared to prevent defectors from returning to Tennessee.

On December 10, those militiamen who sought to return home found their way barred by Jackson, a small body of loyal troops, and two pieces of artillery. "Old Hickory" threatened to shoot the first man who attempted to leave camp, and to show that he meant what he said, he ordered the artillerymen to light their matches in preparation for firing the guns. The mutineers backed down and returned to camp.

A few days later, Cocke arrived at Fort Strother with some fifteen hundred men. Reinforced, Jackson allowed his own volunteers to begin their way home. Soon afterward Cocke informed Jackson that the enlistments of most of his troops would expire in one week and none of his soldiers would be in the field past mid-January 1814. Disheartened, Jackson had even more reason to be concerned when he received a letter from Coffee informing him that many of his troopers had also opted to return home. Coffee could do nothing to prevent them as he had been ill and confined to bed. The new year thus marked a low point for Jackson. "My situation for several weeks past has been exceedingly unpleasant," he wrote, with "discontented troops ... scarcity of provisions and an enemy before me whom I could not advance [against] to conquer." Governor Blount responded to Jackson's request for more militia by suggesting that Jackson return to Tennessee with the "handful of brave men" that remained with him. Jackson, however, was adamant. He remained at Fort Strother with a little over one hundred troops, condemning Blount for not supporting him and swearing that he would either defeat the Creeks or die trying, with or without reinforcements.

A New Year and a Renewed Effort

To date, long distances, fragile communications, rough terrain, and competing visions had made it difficult to coordinate the various independent arms of the American war effort in the South. To improve coordination, in November 1813 Secretary of War Armstrong had directed General Pinckney to leave his headquarters in South Carolina and to travel to Georgia to assume overall command of the war against the Red Sticks.

Rather than take to the field himself, Pinckney chose to provide recommendations and advice to his subordinates for how they could better implement the government's strategy of using converging columns to penetrate the Creek homeland. By the time he was in place and in communication with all of his subordinates, it was too late to impact events in 1813, but his presence would facilitate operations in the new year. His primary contribution was the establishment of more effective communications between the Georgians at Fort Mitchell and Jackson at Fort Strother by using allied Creeks as runners. He also created a company of allied American Indians as scouts, which he attached to Jackson's command.

By mid-January 1814, the Tennesseans and Georgians were ready to embark on a renewed effort. Their ultimate objective was the Red Stick bastion of Tohopeka, a town located on a curve of the Tallapoosa River known as the Horseshoe Bend. Once they captured the town, the combined armies would be positioned to dominate the rest of the Creek heartland. Assisting them would be a third column advancing from Fort Claiborne in the South.

▼ Creek Chief Yoholo Micco was an ally of the American forces during the Creek War. He was known for his gentle and diplomatic manner, and in 1826 was part of a delegation that went to Washington, D.C., to represent the Native American cause. (DeGolyer Library, Southern Methodist University)

A New Year and a Renewed Effort

At Fort Strother, the arrival of the remnants of Coffee's command and about eight hundred new volunteers boosted Jackson's forces to about nine hundred thirty men. Having experienced the disadvantages of campaigning with raw recruits whose enlistments were about to expire, Jackson asked that he be allowed to use the 39th U.S. Infantry, a well-equipped and disciplined regiment then recruiting in East Tennessee. General Flournoy agreed to the request, but Jackson did not have time to wait for its arrival. Pinckney had notified Jackson that the Georgians were about to march, and knowing that he must act before his volunteers' two-month enlistments expired, Jackson broke camp on January 17 and headed south toward the Tallapoosa River without the 39th Infantry. The following day, about two hundred American Indian allies joined his ranks. By the twentieth, Jackson reached Emuckfau Creek, several miles north of Tohopeka.

On the same day that Jackson left Fort Strother, Floyd departed his base at Fort Mitchell with some seventeen hundred militiamen, three hundred allied Creek warriors, and a couple of cannon. On the twentieth, he halted his army to construct Fort Hull as a supply point five miles southeast of present-day Tuskegee, Alabama, and about forty miles south of the Horseshoe Bend. Realizing that they would have no chance should Jackson and Floyd

◀▲ *Major Ridge was a renowned Cherokee military commander. Although as a young man he fought against the American settlers, he eventually allied himself to the United States in the Creek War, and received his "Major" title.* (Museum of Early Southern Decorative Arts)

◀ *Andrew Jackson during the War of 1812*, by Mallon & Hanson. (Library of Congress)

53

▲ The information board and landscape nicely correspond at the historic site of the battle of Horseshoe Bend. The board opens with an uncompromising quote from General Jackson: "Any officer or soldier who flies before the enemy—shall suffer death." (Allen Patterson/CC BY-SA 2.0, via Wikimedia Commons)

◀ Chief Menawa was one of the leading commanders of Red Stick forces during the Creek War. He had a Creek mother and a European father of Scottish ancestry. (PD, via Wikimedia Commons)

A New Year and a Renewed Effort

join forces, the Red Sticks decided to go on the offensive. With Floyd engaged in building Fort Hull, the American Indians opted to strike the most immediate threat.

During the night of January 21, scouts reported to Jackson that the Red Sticks had advanced from Tohopeka and intended to strike him before dawn. The Red Sticks sniped at the camp throughout the night to prevent the Tennesseans from resting. The warriors then mounted a determined predawn attack, which the Americans repulsed. Jackson reported that in the face of a Creek assault, his troops "though raw met their bold and ferocious attack with firmness and undaunted resolution." After dawn, part of Jackson's troops "where the battle waxed hottest" showed signs of breaking. Jackson ordered his small body of reserve troops to bolster the weakening line, and a sudden charge led by Coffee forced the American Indians to leave the field. The Tennesseans repulsed a renewed Red Stick attack later in the day "with stubborn firmness."

▶ James Monroe served as the secretary of state between 1811 and 1817 and the secretary of war between 1814 and 1815. (National Portrait Gallery)

The Creek War, 1813–14

BATTLE OF ENOTICHOPCO.

The Red Sticks did not renew their assault on the Tennesseans' camp on the twenty-second, which gave Jackson time to consider his next move. He received intelligence from his scouts that the Red Sticks had constructed strong defensive works at Tohopeka. In addition, Coffee had suffered a serious wound, and Jackson's nephew and aide, Major Alexander Donelson, had been killed in the fighting. A shortage of supplies exacerbated the situation as well, and Jackson decided to return to Fort Strother.

Jackson began his withdrawal on January 23, with the Red Sticks harassing the column as it retired. After allowing most of the column to cross Enotachopco Creek on January 24, the Red Sticks attacked in force. Jackson had anticipated such a move, however, and had reversed the march of the column, which brought a sizable force to bear along the east bank of the creek. Many of his men fled during the American Indian attack but enough soldiers remained, supported by two artillery pieces, to prevent the Red Stick warriors from crossing the creek. The militiamen then pursued the Red Sticks for several miles.

Following the battle of Enotachopco Creek, the Tennesseans returned to Fort Strother without further incident. Their safe passage reflected a strategic decision on the part of the Red Stick leadership. Having repulsed one arm of

▲ A colorful artwork represents the battle of Enotachopco Creek. An American officer (likely General General Andrew Jackson or General John Coffee), astride his white horse, rallies his troops against the attacks of the Red Sticks. (Tennessee Virtual Archive/PD)

the advancing pincer, the Red Sticks turned to meet the second threat to the Tallapoosa towns, that posed by the Georgians approaching from the south.

After spending several days building Fort Hull, Floyd arrived south of Tohopeka on January 25, the day after the engagement at Enotachopco. Rather than rush to the attack, he stopped to drill his army. He then marched his men a mile and a half on the twenty-sixth only to stop again when he received word of a large Red Stick force moving toward him. Unwilling to risk an open engagement, General

Native American adoption of firearms

The acquisition of firearms changed Native American warfare profoundly. When compared to early firearms, bows and arrows did offer superior performance in some aspects, particularly rate of fire and (in well-trained hands) accuracy, but firearms had a range, power, and effect that could not be denied. Thus firearms of all types—muskets, rifles, and handguns—became increasingly sought after among many Native American tribes from the 17th and 18th centuries.

As the Native Americans did not have the capabilities or materials for indigenous firearms production, access to guns and ammunition came through trade. Given that the Native Americans were frequently at war with the settlers, the firearm trade routes could be convoluted. Firearms were often purchased from foreign importers, gun traders from Britain, Spain, or France, for example. They might also be bought from another American Indian tribe, one that already had good trading relations with the settlers and had built up stockpiles of firearms for sale. Often, however, guns, cartridges, and gun-smithing support (the latter was especially important) were acquired directly from the settler communities, usually swapped for valuable commodities such as beaver pelts and buffalo hides. Even when there were severe prohibitions on sales, the Native Americans could usually find willing intermediaries, not least because the American Indian peoples were profitable and scalable customers. Furthermore, firearms might be transferred as part of a diplomatic exchange.

The adoption of firearms changed not only Native American ways of war, but also, to a degree, Native American culture. Guns became status symbols, imbued with mystical significance. The competent handling and maintenance of firearms became integral to the expression of manhood. Guns also gave birth to new indigenous art forms, the Native American women producing accessories such as cartridge belts and gun slips.

The Creek War, 1813–14

Floyd chose to construct a fortified encampment dubbed Camp Defiance, on Calabee Creek.

The Red Sticks struck Camp Defiance during the predawn hours of January 27. About thirteen hundred warriors crept through the swamps of Calabee Creek undetected. When they reached the sentinels, they fired on them and rushed into the camp. Completely surprised, the pickets nevertheless made a stout resistance behind barricades, giving time for the rest of the troops to fall into the formations Floyd had taught them two days earlier. The Georgians soon realized that they could not maneuver effectively within the small encampment. Fortunately for them, daybreak allowed them to target the Red Stick warriors more effectively. Supported by their artillery, the Georgians gained the advantage and the Red Sticks withdrew.

Floyd's losses were terrible for the Creek War, twenty-five killed and one hundred fifty wounded. The attack had wrought so much damage that the Georgians and their Creek allies spent the next six days recuperating. Floyd and his army then limped back to Fort Hull. With the enlistments of many of his militiamen about to expire, the general left a small garrison at Fort Hull under

▶ An exquisitely rendered portrait of a Creek warrior by the artist John Trumbull. The figure, Hopothle Mico, was likely drawn at the signing of the Treaty of New York on August 7, 1790. (John Trumbull/PD, via Wikimedia Commons)

▼ An example of Creek wall art, depicting a mythical combat. Although the Creeks kept many of their traditional ways of life, they also readily absorbed cultural influences from the European settlers. (DrStew82/CC BY-SA 4.0, via Wikimedia Commons)

Hopothle Mico — or the Talassee King of the Creeks — J.T. New York 1790

the command of Colonel Homer Milton and brought the rest of the force back to Fort Mitchell where much of it disbanded. Although they had suffered heavy losses, the Red Sticks had by aggressive action defeated each of the two thrusts directed at Tohopeka.

As Jackson's and Floyd's columns recoiled, the third column, unaware of their fate, got under way. In early February, Colonel Russell and his regiment of six hundred regulars departed Fort Claiborne on the lower Alabama River to attack the Old Towns located on the Cahaba River. Rather than use supply wagons, Russell sent a barge loaded with supplies to rendezvous with his column. He intended for the barge, commanded by Captain James Dinkins, to meet him and his troops at the Old Towns. Somehow, Dinkins missed the turnoff for the Cahaba River and did not make the rendezvous. Though the troops moved quickly without the encumbrance of wagons, the Red Sticks still learned of Russell's advance and abandoned the towns. Lacking supplies, the troops lingered in the Old Towns for two days, destroying them before beginning the return march to Fort Claiborne. Russell's winter expedition marked the last U.S. military operation against hostile Creeks in the southern part of the Mississippi Territory.

Andrew Jackson and the Final Campaign

Back at Fort Strother, Jackson busied himself with preparations for a new offensive. In addition to gathering supplies, the general received most welcome reinforcements on February 6 when Major Lemuel P. Montgomery arrived at the head of the 39th Infantry. About twenty-five hundred volunteers from Tennessee also arrived that week. Meanwhile, Pinckney informed Jackson that he was organizing new columns to advance from Forts Claiborne and Mitchell in a reprise of the January campaign.

After having gathered a sufficient quantity of supplies, Jackson marched out of Fort Strother on March 14 with twenty-two hundred infantry, Coffee's seven hundred mounted troops, and six hundred American Indian allies (five hundred Cherokees and one hundred National Creeks). The army also had two cannon, a 6-pounder and a 3-pounder. The troops moved south along the Coosa River with the 39th Infantry following the bank of the river guarding the supply barges. About sixty miles from Fort Strother, Jackson halted his army and built a supply post named Fort Williams.

On March 24, Jackson's column left Fort Williams and approached Tohopeka after a three-day march. What Jackson found impressed him. "It is difficult to conceive a situation more eligible for defense than the one they had chosen," he reported to Pinckney. At the large bend of the river, the Red Sticks had built across the peninsula a zigzag log fortification, five to eight feet high, which could allow them to enfilade attackers as they got close to the wall. The Red Sticks had constructed the barricade so that their fire could be delivered through loopholes, minimizing their exposure to enemy musket fire. Menewa, "the Great Warrior," acted as overall Red Stick commander at Horseshoe Bend.

Jackson, "determining to extinguish them," wanted to encircle the Red Sticks so none could flee the area and continue the war if defeated. Accordingly, he

The Creek War, 1813–14

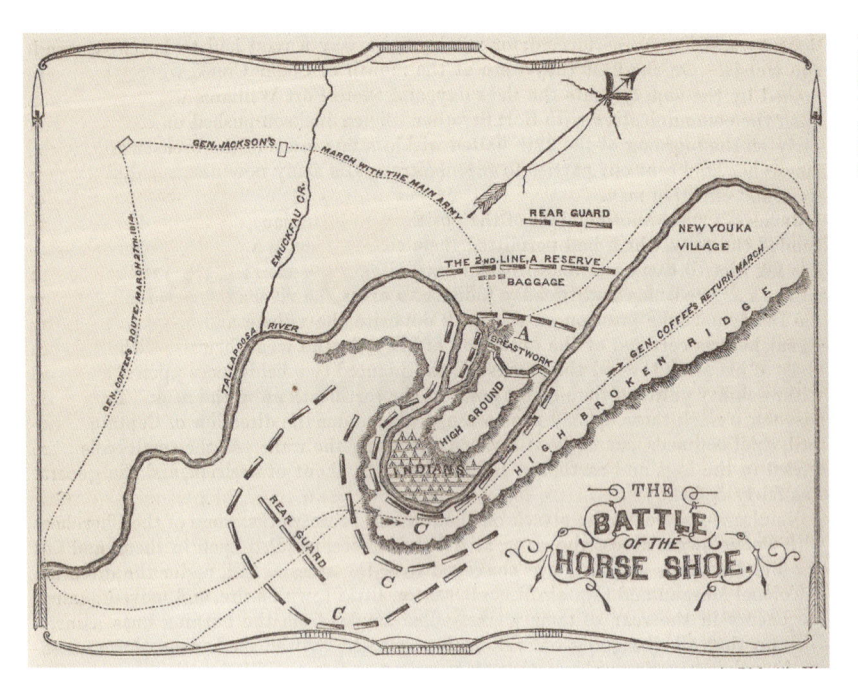

◀ Battle plan of Horseshoe Bend, from Benson John Lossing's *The Pictorial Field-Book of the War of 1812*. (John Frost/PD, via Wikimedia Commons)

◀ An engraving of the battle of Horseshoe Bend shows U.S. troops of the 39th U.S. Infantry making a bayonet charge against the outer defenses of the Red Stick camp. The soldiers ultimately overwhelmed the Native American force, killing c. 800 of them. (New York Public Library)

Andrew Jackson and the Final Campaign

sent Coffee with his mounted volunteers and American Indian allies to line the southern bank of the Tallapoosa River to cut off the enemy's line of retreat. He deployed his main force with the 39th Infantry in the center and the two regiments of Tennessee volunteers on either flank. At 1030, he "planted" his two

▶▼ The Tallapoosa River was one of the key natural features around which the Creek War was fought. It runs a total of 265 miles from the southern Appalachian mountains through Georgia and into Alabama, draining into four lakes along the way. It forms the eponymous bend of Horseshoe Bend National Military Park. (National Park Service)

The Creek War, 1813–14

artillery pieces on an eminence about eighty yards from the barricade and had his chief engineer direct a point-blank artillery barrage on the center of the barricade. The Red Sticks attempted to shoot down the artillery crews, but the American troops laid down such a suppressing fire that the Red Sticks could not aim effectively. After a two-hour bombardment, the artillery had caused only a few casualties among the Red Sticks and only minimal damage to the barricade itself.

To the south of Horseshoe Bend, the impetuous Cherokee warriors became impatient listening to the artillery fire. Many swam the waters of the Tallapoosa River under a covering fire from their comrades. Once on the south bank, they captured the canoes the Red Sticks had left at the riverbank. Soon about one hundred fifty to two hundred National Creeks under William McIntosh and many of Coffee's volunteers crossed the river as well, capturing the town and setting it on fire. They then advanced into the wooded hills that lay between the town and the rear of the barricade. With the barricade's defenders now surrounded, Jackson ordered his infantry to storm the defenses.

At about 1230, the drums of the 39th Infantry began to beat the long roll to arms. Major Montgomery took the lead with his regiment in the center and the Tennessee volunteers on either flank, the whole looking like a large wedge of troops. "The spirit which animated them was a sure augury of the success which was to follow," Jackson observed. Montgomery reached the barricade first, but fell with a bullet to the head. In an instant, the entire 39th had mounted the barricade and became embroiled in savage hand-to-hand combat with the Red Sticks, "in the midst of a most tremendous fire." One of the first to make it over the barricade was Ensign (Third Lieutenant) Sam Houston. Moments after entering the Creek position, Houston received an arrow in his upper thigh, piercing the groin and taking him out of the action.

The Red Sticks fought fiercely, but they were soon overwhelmed. They fled the breastwork and scattered throughout the peninsula. Many made their way to the Tallapoosa and attempted to cross it, but Coffee's volunteers and American

▲ A portrait of the Tennessee politician and diplomat John Williams (1778–1837). As well as helping to recruit and organize the 39th U.S. Infantry, he fought with them at the battle of Horseshoe Bend. (PD, via Wikimedia Commons)

Profile:
Sam Houston (1793–1863)

Sam Houston lived a quite extraordinary life from his early years until his death in 1863. He was born into a log cabin and a large family on March 2, 1793, in Timber Ridge, Virginia. After the death of his father in 1807, his family moved to Maryville, Tennessee, where they collectively farmed and ran a store. At the age of 16, however, Sam ran away and sought to live with the local Cherokees, who adopted him and bestowed on him the Cherokee name "Black Raven." By the age of 19, however, he was back in Maryville.

Houston entered military service during the War of 1812, and served in the Creek War. His ability to understand Native American culture and language proved invaluable during the campaign. He was twice wounded in the battle of Horseshoe Bend. After the war, Houston diversified his skills and experience. He found employment as a subagent managing the removal of the Cherokee from Tennessee to a reservation in the Arkansas Territory, then studied law and passed the bar exam, setting up a legal practice in Nashville. From 1823 to 1827, Houston served as a Democratic Party U.S. congressman and was elected governor of Tennessee in 1827, although he resigned from this post in 1829 and, following a failed marriage, went back to live with the Cherokee in Arkansas Territory.

By 1833, the itinerant Houston was living in Texas. In 1836, he was a signatory on the Texas Declaration of Independence from Mexico and was appointed the commander-in-chief of the Texan army, leading his men to victory at the battle of San Jacinto on April 21, 1836. The celebrated Houston was elected president of the Texas Republic on September 5, 1836, and later became the U.S. state's senator and governor. In 1861, however, Houston fell out of favor in Texas for his refusal to back secession. He was deposed as governor in March 1861, and died at his home two years later.

▼ Sam Houston, here photographed late in his senior years, was a junior officer during the Creek War, where he was wounded. Later in life, a general in rank, he defended Texas against Santa Anna's Mexican forces in 1836 and became president of the Lone Star Republic (Texas). (Mathew Brady/PD, via Wikimedia Commons)

The Creek War, 1813–14

Indian allies ensured that few Red Sticks made it to the opposite bank alive. It took five hours for the volunteers and regulars to hunt down the surviving enemy warriors, with Jackson writing to his wife that "it was dark before we finished killing them." The next day, his men counted 557 enemy warriors "left dead upon the peninsula," not counting the several hundred casualties inflicted by Coffee's command. Only about 200 of the 1,000 defenders escaped. Jackson and his American Indian allies suffered about 260 casualties. The victors also rounded up some 350 women and children as prisoners. Jackson later boasted that "the history of warfare furnishes few instances of a more brilliant attack."

After securing the prisoners and tending to the wounded, Jackson turned his army toward Fort Williams. From there he could plan the next phase of the war. He believed that the remaining Red Stick warriors would regroup near the confluence of the Coosa and Tallapoosa Rivers, about forty miles from the Horseshoe Bend. Expecting to be joined soon by a new militia army advancing from Georgia under the command of Colonel Milton and Colonel Russell's 3d Infantry from Fort Claiborne, Jackson intended to sweep the country of the lower Coosa River from Fort Williams to the old Fort Toulouse site (near modern Montgomery) to eliminate all resistance. Jackson set his sights on the last major Red Stick stronghold at Othlewallee on the Tallapoosa River, near present-day Wetumpka, Alabama. He thought Weatherford, who had not been at Horseshoe Bend, might make a stand there. He wanted to march his army down the Tallapoosa River to the Hickory Ground while having Milton's force, marching from Fort Hull, join him along the way. Although short on supplies, Jackson

◀ *Interview between Gen. Jackson & Weatherford*, engraving by John Reuben Chapin, depicting Weatherford's surrender after the battle of Horseshoe Bend. (Library of Congress)

Andrew Jackson and the Final Campaign

had been reassured by General Pinckney that Milton had stockpiled sufficient provisions at Fort Hull to support the operation, and Colonel Russell was to advance supplies up from the south as well.

On April 7, Jackson began his march with the 39th Infantry, over six hundred fifty mounted Tennesseans under Coffee, and almost two thousand Tennessee volunteers. Six days later, he reached Fushatchee on the Tallapoosa River and found it deserted. He also found Othlewallee deserted. After putting both towns to the torch, Jackson marched his troops toward the Hickory Ground. By the time he reached it on April 17, Milton had already arrived. Jackson had his troops build another fortification on the site of old Fort Toulouse, which they named Fort Jackson in his honor.

The absence of further resistance signaled an end to the Creek War. Secretary of War

▲ William Blount. (New York Public Library)

▶ This scene shows the Creek leaders negotiating the Treaty of Fort Jackson in 1814, although in reality the terms of the treaty were imposed upon the Native Americans, including those who had fought as allies of the settlers. (New York Public Library)

The Creek War, 1813–14

◀ This artwork, created in 1847, gives an impression of the battle of Pensacola (1814), specifically the destruction of Fort Barrancas by the British. General Andrew Jackson's U.S. troops advance across the water. (John Frost/PD, via Wikimedia Commons)

Armstrong selected General Pinckney to represent the United States in peace negotiations with the Creeks, with Hawkins as his adviser. Pinckney ordered Jackson to march his troops back to Tennessee, and "Old Hickory" arrived at Nashville in May with most of his men. Soon thereafter, the now-famous Jackson received a brevet major general's commission in the U.S. Army and command of the 7th Military District. The government also made him its representative at the

▼ Horseshoe Bend National Military Park, in Tallapoosa County, Alabama, maintains the site at which Major General Andrew Jackson's 3,300 U.S. soldiers attacked Chief Menawa's 1,000 Red Stick Creek warriors. (Allen Patterson/CC BY-SA 2.0, via Wikimedia Commons)

Militia in the War of 1812

Militia forces were at the heart of the U.S. war effort during the War of 1812. In total, about 528,000 American soldiers fought in the conflict; 458,000 of those served in the state militias. But the scale of the militia was generally inverse to its quality. Although there were many effective militia units and leaders during the War of 1812, on the whole the militia forces were of poor quality compared to federal units. The responsibility for training and equipping militia units fell upon the shoulders of the state governments, many of which simply neglected to invest seriously or properly, or even actively resisted for a variety of political or logistical reasons. The consequences were felt most acutely by the militia soldiers on the front line. They were usually extremely poorly paid; government pay for a militia private volunteer was about $5 per month, compared to up to $12 per month for a laborer; the government tried to balance this out by offering land incentives. Training was frequently inadequate, weapons and equipment were often substandard, and food could be scarce and poor, all factors that raised casualties and lowered morale on campaign. Commanders were often inexperienced, and not unusually incompetent. The consequence was that, while acknowledging the bravery and skill of some, many militia units struggled to perform convincingly on the battlefield. It was for this reason that the U.S. government began to increase its focus on professional federal forces in the postwar years.

▶ The British flee Pensacola as Jackson approaches. (John Frost, Andrew Jackson's Hermitage, 1847)

CREEK NATION
1814

Territory ceded by the Treaty of Fort Jackson

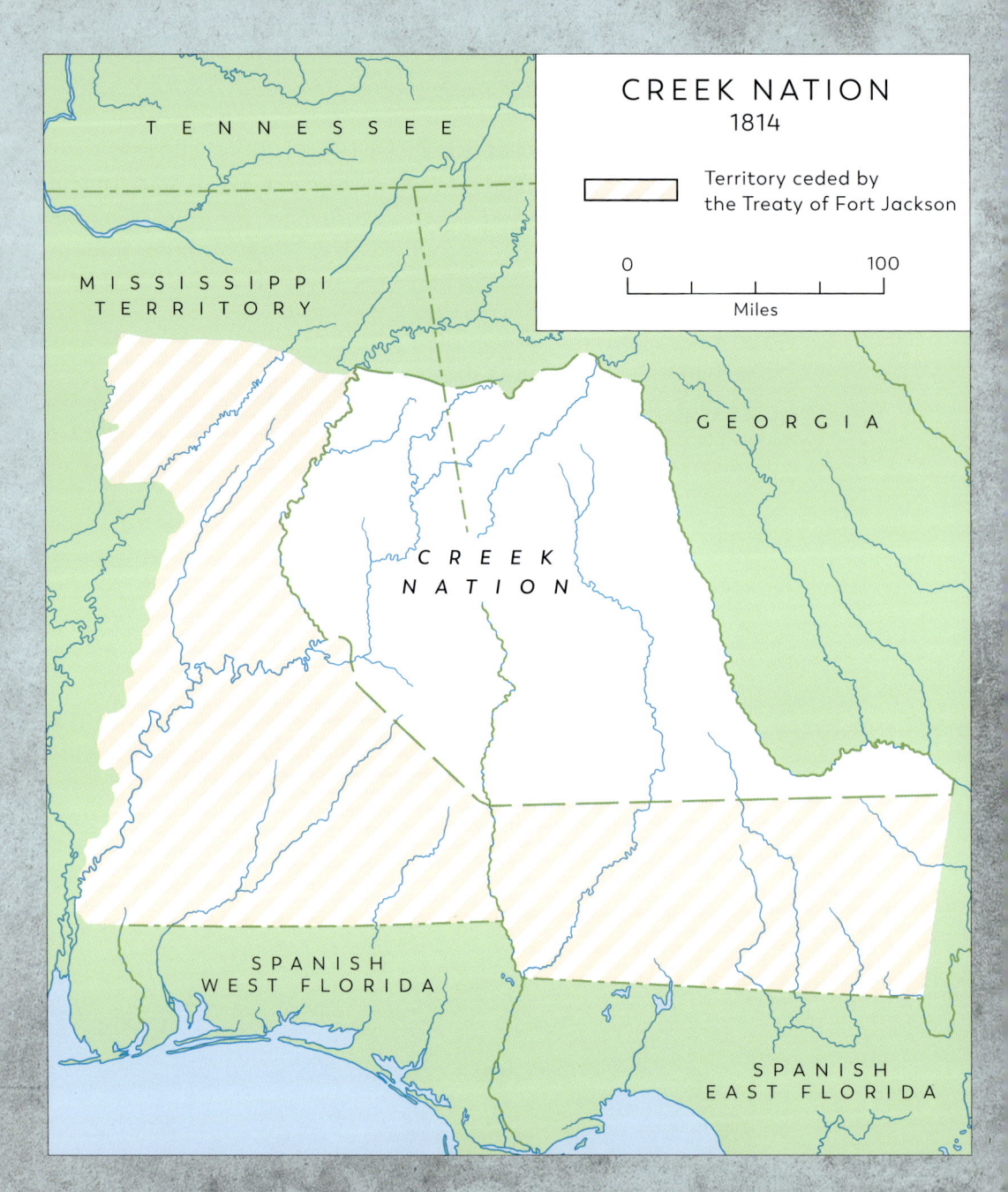

0 — 100 Miles

TENNESSEE

MISSISSIPPI TERRITORY

GEORGIA

CREEK NATION

SPANISH WEST FLORIDA

SPANISH EAST FLORIDA

▲ Map 3

upcoming treaty conference instead of Pinckney. In July, the Tennessean ordered Hawkins to have all the Creek headmen meet at Fort Jackson on August 1, 1814.

The federal government dictated to Jackson what the terms of the peace treaty would be. The Creeks would have to cede enough land to pay for the expenses of the war (Map 3). Since the Spanish had supplied the Red Sticks, the Creeks could have no further interaction with them and trade only with the United States. Furthermore, the Creeks had to grant the United States the right to build roads, forts, and trading posts, and to have free navigation of all waterways through their remaining territory. Last, the Creeks had to turn over all the surviving Red Stick leaders, including the religious prophets whom the United States held responsible for inciting the war.

▶ A letter written by Andrew Jackson on July 12, 1814 discussing the current situation. (Library of Congress)

The Creek War, 1813–14

At the treaty negotiations, Jackson stunned the Creek headmen by adding to the list of concessions a requirement of his own—the cession of 23 million acres of land, fully one-half of the Creek territory. He made no distinction between those Creeks who had been his allies and those who had fought against the United States. The Creek headmen rejected the demand, but Jackson was adamant. After delaying for a week, the Creek headmen realized that they could not resist him further, especially with his army still in the field. On August 9, 1814, the thirty-six Creek headmen present signed the treaty. Because of his unyielding manner in obtaining the harsh terms, the Creeks dubbed Jackson "Sharp Knife."

The treaty signing occurred just in time. Several days later, a British expedition arrived in the Gulf of Mexico at the Apalachicola River and in Pensacola. With the Creek War at an end, Jackson could turn his full attention to the new adversary. He marched his army to Mobile where he repelled a British attack in mid-September 1814. He then marched to Pensacola and forced the British to withdraw completely from the Gulf Coast. Anticipating a British attack on New Orleans, he then marched to Louisiana, giving Pensacola back to the Spanish.

Analysis

The volunteer militias of Georgia, Tennessee, and the Mississippi Territory bore the brunt of the Creek War. Augmenting them were two regiments of regulars, the 3d and the 39th U.S. Infantry; and friendly Choctaws, Cherokees, and Creeks who, while outnumbered by the militia, nevertheless played important roles in determining the outcome of the conflict.

In terms of combat effectiveness, the volunteer militia proved brave if inexperienced and undisciplined. The greatest handicap posed by the militiamen was their frequent unwillingness to serve for longer than their initial term of enlistment, which was often six months and sometimes less. Short-term enlistments became serious obstacles since the tasks of raising, organizing, and moving a force into the Red Stick territory; establishing supply points; and conducting operations proved time consuming. This was particularly true given the daunting terrain, which ranged from swamps and creeks in the lower Mississippi Territory to the mountains of northern Alabama, with few roads on which to bring in supplies. Inclement weather also impeded progress, especially during winter when soldiers frequently lacked proper shelter and camp equipment. Taken together, short enlistments, inadequate logistical arrangements, and the challenges posed by terrain and weather hamstrung many American operations.

During the Creek War, the Americans followed a strategy that they had often employed against American Indians east of the Mississippi River. Targeting American Indian settlements forced the Red Sticks to make difficult choices—either they could stand and fight to protect their property at the risk of suffering heavy casualties in battle or they could abandon their settlements, avoiding casualties but losing the shelter, property, and food stores that the towns provided, particularly in winter. Whatever course the American Indians chose, over time they would suffer sufficient attrition in either men or resources to break their will to resist. Using several columns to converge simultaneously on the Creek heartland only magnified the dilemma facing Red Stick leaders.

The Creek War, 1813–14

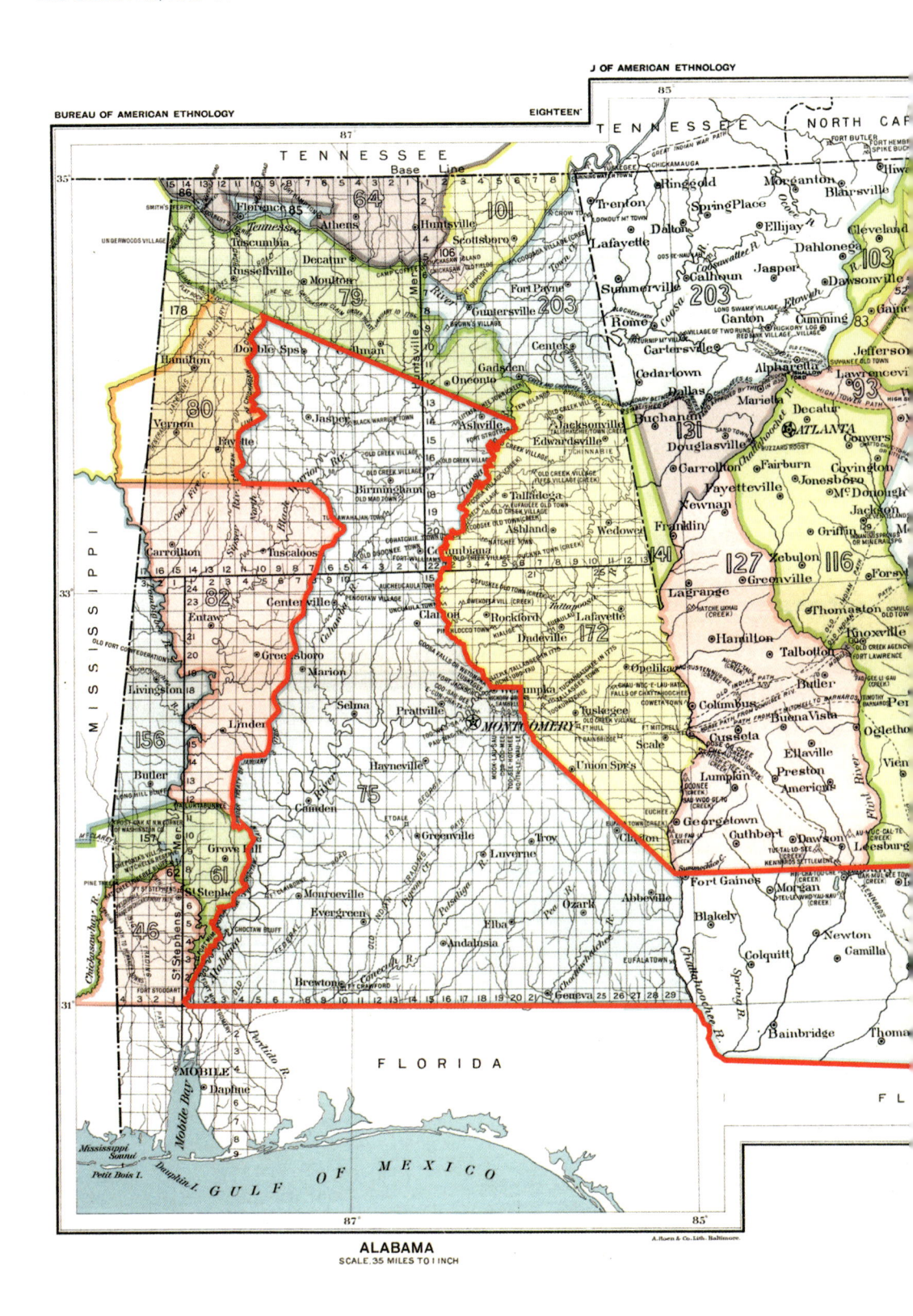

Though their strategy was fundamentally sound, American commanders found that it was difficult to execute given all the impediments enumerated above. Poor communications and loose command arrangements further increased the challenges. Personal rivalries prevented Jackson and Cocke from waging a successful combined campaign in 1813, while communication obstacles impeded the coordination of the Tennesseans' movements with those of the Georgians and Mississippians. The appointment of General Pinckney as overall commander somewhat reduced but did not overcome the barriers to successful coordination. In January 1814, Floyd and Jackson came close to affecting a juncture at Tohopeka, but sufficient time and space between their movements allowed the Red Sticks to exploit their central position and to repulse each of the columns in turn. Had the movements of Jackson and Floyd been more in sync, or had Tohopeka's defenders not responded to the converging threat aggressively, the war might have ended a few months earlier than it did.

Taking to the offensive also seemed to be the best tactic for the Red Sticks. When on the attack as at Fort Mims and at Calabee, Emuckfau, and Enotachopco Creeks, they emerged victorious either by inflicting more casualties or by turning back the advancing Americans. When the Red Sticks remained on the defensive, allowing the Americans to attack them in their towns, they usually

◀ A map showing the settlement of the Treaty of Fort Jackson (August 9, 1814) that ended the Creek War. The treaty was territorially punishing for the Creek Nation, which ceded nearly twenty-two million acres of its ancestral lands to the United States. (Wtfiv/LOC)

incurred stinging defeats. It is curious then why they allowed themselves to be attacked at Tohopeka in March 1814. Notwithstanding its impressive fortifications, the town proved to be a deathtrap for the Red Sticks.

Total deaths for U.S. forces, regulars and militia, are estimated at 575. About 1,600 Red Stick warriors died. Many American Indian civilians died of starvation or disease brought on by the loss of their homes in winter. While some Creeks moved westward or into Florida after 1814, most stayed on their greatly diminished territory in present-day Alabama. In 1832, the Treaty of Cusseta transferred the ownership of Creek lands from the tribe to individual American Indians. Sales by the owners of these individual allotments to white settlers and land speculators, as well as illegal encroachment, caused continued friction and eventually sparked the Second Creek War of 1836. The conflict provided Jackson, now president of the United States, with the pretext to force all of the remaining Creeks to emigrate to Indian Territory (modern-day Oklahoma) west of the Mississippi River during August and September 1836.

Further Reading

Benn, Carl. *The War of 1812*. Oxford: Osprey Publishing, 2024.

Black, Jeremy. *The War of 1812 in the Age of Napoleon*. London: Continuum, 2010.

Bunn, Mike, and Clay Williams. *Battle for the Southern Frontier: The Creek War and the War of 1812*. Charleston, S.C.: History Press, 2008.

Cozzens, Peter. *A Brutal Reckoning: The Creek Indians and the Epic War for the American South*. London: Atlantic Books, 2024.

Cozzens, Peter. *The Warrior and the Prophet: The Epic Story of the Brothers Who Led the Native American Resistance*. London: Atlantic Books, 2022.

Esposito, Gabriele. *Armies of the War of 1812: The Armies of the United States, United Kingdom and Canada from 1812 to 1815*. Point Pleasant, NJ: Winged Hussar Publishing, 2019.

Gregg, Adams. *US Soldier vs British Soldier: War of 1812*. Oxford: Osprey Publishing, 2021.

Griffith, Benjamin W., Jr. *McIntosh and Weatherford, Creek Indian Leaders*. Tuscaloosa: University of Alabama Press, 1988.

Halbert, Henry S., and T. H. Ball. *The Creek War of 1813 and 1814*. Chicago: Donohue & Henneberry, 1895.

Holland, James W. *Andrew Jackson and the Creek War: Victory at Horseshoe Bend*. Tuscaloosa: University of Alabama Press, 1990.

Kochan, James. *The United States Army 1783–1811*. Oxford: Osprey Publishing, 2001.

Owsley, Frank Lawrence, Jr. *Struggle for the Gulf Borderlands: The Creek War and the Battle of New Orleans, 1812–1815*. Gainesville: University Presses of Florida, 1981.

Smith, Gene Allen. *The Slaves' Gamble: Choosing Sides in the War of 1812*. New York: Palgrave Macmillan, 2013.

Stewart, Richard W. (ed.). *American Military History, Volume I: The United States Army and the Forging of a Nation*. Washington, D.C: US Army Center of Military History, 2005.

Taylor, Alan. *The Civil War of 1812: American Citizens, British Subjects, Irish Rebels, & Indian Allies.* New York: Vintage Books, 2011.

Waselkov, Gregory A. *A Conquering Spirit: Fort Mims and the Red Stick War of 1813–1814.* Tuscaloosa: University of Alabama Press, 2006.

Weir, Howard T. *A Paradise of Blood: The Creek War of 1813–14.* Yardley, PA: Westholme Publishing, 2016.

Index

Adams, Maj. Gen. David, 42, 45
Agriculture, 10
Alabama River, 8, 20, 21, 25, 44, 47, 60
Ambushes, 44, 46
American Indian, 9, 12, 14, 16, 43, 52, 53, 55, 56, 57, 63, 66, 73, 76
    chiefs/leaders, 10, 12, 16, 18, 20, 42, 47, 67, 71, 73
        Latecau, 19
        Little Warrior, 16, 17
        McQueen, Peter (Red Stick leader), 8, 20, 23
        Pushmataha (Choctaw chief), 14, 44–48
        Tecumseh (Shawnee warrior), 6, 13–14, 16, 17, 19
        Tenskwatawa ("the Prophet"), 12
        Weatherford, William (Red Stick leader), 8, 33, 47, 48, 66
    tribes, 9, 14, 37, 43, 57
        Cherokees, 38, 61, 65, 73
        Choctaws, 14, 48, 73
        Creeks, 6, 9–12, 16, 17, 18, 20, 26, 28, 29, 32–33, 35, 38, 41, 42, 45, 52, 60, 68, 71–72, 73, 76
        Lower, 9–12
        National, 19, 20, 61, 64
        Upper, 9–11
        Red Sticks, 8, 16, 18, 19, 20, 23, 25, 26, 28, 29, 32, 33, 40–43, 46–47, 49, 52, 55–60, 61, 64–66, 71, 73–76
ammunition, 18, 20, 47, 57
    cartridges, 57
    gunpowder, 20
    lead, 20
Apalachicola River, 72
Armstrong, Secretary of War John, 16, 17, 29, 52, 67–68

artillery, 8, 20, 51, 56, 58, 64
    cannon, 41, 50, 53, 61
        3-pounder, 61
        6-pounder, 61
Autossee (Red Stick town), 8, 24, 41, 42, 44

Bailey, Capt. Dixon, 26, 28
battles of
    Burnt Corn Creek, 6, 7, 20–24
    Econochaca/Holy Ground, 8, 45–47
    Enotachopco Creek, 56, 75
    Horseshoe Bend, 6, 8, 54, 62, 64, 65
    Pensacola, 68, 69, 72
    San Jacinto, 65
    Talladega, 6, 8, 34, 35–36, 38
    Tallushatchee, 8, 32, 33, 34, 35, 38, 40
    Tohopeka, 55, 56, 57–60, 61, 75, 76
Beasley, Maj. Daniel, 25–26
Black Warrior River, 31, 48
Blount, Governor William, 7, 16–17, 29–30, 49, 51, 67
Burnt Corn Creek, 22, 23, 24, 44

Cahaba River, 24, 60
Calabee Creek, 24, 58
Caller, Col. James, 6, 7, 20–23
Camp Defiance, 8, 58
Carson, Col. Joseph, 44–46
cavalry, 17, 21, 30, 31, 33, 43
ceremonies (and dances), 19, 20
Chattahoochee River, 8, 41
"civilization program," 6, 10
Claiborne, Brig. Gen. Ferdinand L., 8, 21, 25–27, 44–48, 49
Cocke, Maj. Gen. John A., 30, 32, 33, 38, 51, 75

Coffee, Brig. Gen. John, 8, 17–18, 30–32, 34–35, 39, 40, 51, 53, 55–56, 61, 63, 64, 66
Coosa (Creek town), 15, 19, 24
Coosa River, 9, 15, 18, 31, 32, 61, 66
councils, 11, 14, 16, 18, 19, 29
Coweta (Lower Creek capital), 15, 18, 24, 41
Creek Nation, 6, 7, 9, 10, 16, 18, 74–75

Dale, Capt. Samuel, 20, 21
defectors, 51
Dinkins, Capt. James, 60
disease, 40, 76
Duck River, 16

Eccanachaca, or the Holy Ground, 8, 44–47
Emuckfau Creek, 53, 75
enlistments, 44, 48, 49, 51, 53, 58, 73
Enotachopco Creek, 56–57, 75
Eustis, Secretary of War William, 16
expeditions, 16–17, 29, 30, 60, 72

federal government, 71
Federal Road, 6, 12, 14–16, 24, 40
Flint River, 15, 40
Floyd, Brig. Gen. John, 31, 40–42, 44, 49, 53, 55, 57–58, 60, 75
formations, 43, 46, 58
Fort Claiborn, 24, 44, 48, 52, 60, 66
Fort Deposit, 24, 31, 38–39, 45, 49
Fort Hull, 24, 53, 55, 57, 58, 66–67
Fort Lawrence, 15, 40–41
Fort Leslie, 33
Fort Mims, 6, 8
    massacre at, 7, 25–58
Fort Mitchell, 8, 24, 41, 42, 50, 52, 53, 60

79

Fort Strother, 24, 32–33, 38, 39, 49, 51, 52, 53, 56, 61
Fort Toulouse (site later renamed Fort Jackson), 24, 66, 67, 70, 71, 74–75
Fort Williams, 24, 61, 66

garrisons, 25, 26, 28, 50, 58
Gulf Coast, 6, 14, 72

Hawkins, Benjamin (American Indian agent for the United States), 9, 10–11, 16, 18, 29, 41, 68, 71
headquarters, 40, 52
Hickory Ground, 24, 31, 66, 67
Horseshoe Bend, 24, 52, 53, 61, 63, 64, 66, 68
Houston, Ensign (Third Lt.) Sam, 64–65
Huntsville, 15, 24, 30, 31, 39, 51

infantry, 17, 31, 33, 43, 61, 64

Jackson, Maj. Gen. Andrew "Old Hickory," 6–8, 17, 29–35, 38–39, 44, 45, 49, 51, 52–56, 61, 64, 66–69, 71–72, 75, 76

letters, 17, 20, 29, 33, 47, 51, 71

Madison, President James, 16
marches, 31, 33, 39, 40–41, 45, 48, 53, 56, 57, 60, 61, 66–68, 72
market economy, 11
massacre at Fort Mims, 6, 7, 25–28
military districts
    6th Military District, 40
    7th Military District, 17, 39, 68
militia
    East Tennessee, 8, 32, 33, 38, 51
    Fayetteville, 31
    Georgia, 8, 29, 40–43
    Mississippi, 44–48
    Tennessee, 8, 32, 33, 38, 51
Milton, Col. Homer, 60, 66, 67
Mississippi River, 17, 73, 76
Mississippi Territory, 8, 12, 17, 20, 25, 31, 39, 44, 200
Mitchell, Governor David B., 7, 29, 40, 61
Mobile, Alabama, 8, 14, 15, 24, 29, 44, 47, 72

fall of, 17–18
port of, 16
Montgomery, Maj. Lemuel P., 61, 64
murders, 17
mutineers/mutinies, 44, 49, 51

Nashville, 17, 30, 65, 68
Natchez (Mississippi River town), 15, 17
    trail (known as the Natchez Trace), 17
National Council (governing body of all Creeks), 11, 14, 16, 29, 35

Ocmulgee River, 6, 10, 15
Oconee River, 9, 15
Ogeechee River, 9, 15
Ohio River, 17
Okfuskee, 15, 19, 24
Othlewallee, 24, 66, 67

pan-American Indian alliance, 6, 14, 16
peace negotiations, 68
Pensacola, 15, 18, 20, 24, 44, 72
    port of, 16
pickets, 58
pincer movements, 29, 56–57
Pinckney, Maj. Gen. Thomas, 40–42, 52, 53, 61, 67, 68, 75

rear guard, 42
reinforcements, 20, 39, 51, 61
rivalries, 75
runners, 52
Russell, Col. Gilbert C., 44, 48, 60, 66–67

scouts, 20, 45, 52, 55, 56
Second Creek War of 1836, 76
sentinels, 58
settlements, 9, 20, 21, 25, 26, 41, 73, 75
shortages, 40, 44, 49, 56
sieges, 41
slaughter, 35, 38
Smoot, Maj. Benjamin, 44, 46–47
Southern frontier, 16
Spain, 9, 14, 16, 57
starvation, 76
supplies, 20, 23, 33, 38–39, 40, 42, 44, 56, 60, 61, 66–67, 73

supply barges, 60, 61
supply wagons, 32, 60

tactics (American Indian), 21, 43
Talladega, 24, 33
Tallapoosa River, 8, 9, 15, 18, 24, 31, 33, 41, 42, 46, 52, 53, 63, 64, 66, 67
Tallushatchee, 24, 32
Tennessee River, 31, 32, 39
Tensaw District, 20, 25, 48
threats, 38, 43, 51, 55, 57, 75
Tohopeka (Red Stick town), 24, 52, 55, 56
tolls, 12
Tombigbee River, 15, 24, 25
trading posts, 14, 71
treaties, 9, 10
    1805 treaty, 12
    Treaty of Cusseta, 76
    Treaty of Fort Jackson, 6, 8, 67, 70, 74–75
Tuckabatchee (national Creek capital), 15, 18, 24

U.S. forces, 76
    3d Infantry Regiment, 7, 29, 44, 45, 47, 48, 66
    39th Infantry Regiment, 53, 61, 62, 63, 64, 67, 73

victories, 9, 32, 34, 38, 47, 65
volunteers, 7, 17, 53, 63, 64, 66, 69, 73
    Tennessee, 49–51, 61, 63, 64, 67

weapons
    atlatl, 37
    bayonet, 21, 42, 62
    blade, 37, 38–39
    clubs, 37
        ball-headed, 37
        gunstock war, 37
        stone, 37
        wooden, 37
    daggers, 37, 39
    muskets, 39, 50, 57
    rifles, 20, 35, 57
    shotguns, 20
    war hatchets, 37
White, Brig. Gen. James, 8, 33, 38
Wilkinson, Maj. Gen. James, 17–18